The 'Accidental' Presidents

who Became

The 'Blessers' of Israel

To Dow

God Bless you

John Somerville

Colonel John T. Somerville USMC (Ret.)

ISBN: 978-965-7542-72-9

Editing and Lay-out:
Petra van der Zande, Tsur Tsina Publications, Jerusalem, Israel.
Editing: Linda Smith, USA
Cover artwork Mt. Rushmore: Vinícius Rosa de Almeida

Photos, maps and illustrations:
internet, John Somerville personal collection

Contact information:
John T. Somerville
P.O. Box 664
North Fork, CA 93643, USA
Email: israel4somerville@gmail.com
Website: www.israelsomerville.com

Order information:
Email: israel4somerville@gmail.com
Or website: www.lulu.com

Zion's Watchmen, a non-profit 501 (c) 3 incorporated in Texas, committed to the biblical mandate to bless, speak out and stand with Israel and the Jewish people.

Table of Contents

Golda Meir Quotes

♦   *We have always said that in our war with the Arabs we had a secret weapon - no alternative.*
♦   *To be or not to be is not a question of compromise. Either you be or you don't be.*
♦   *We do not rejoice in victories. We rejoice when a new kind of cotton is grown and when strawberries bloom in Israel.*
♦   *The Egyptians could run to Egypt, the Syrians into Syria. The only place we could run was into the sea, and before we did that we might as well fight.*

INTRODUCTION

This book showcases a few American presidents who were totally unqualified to be presidents and logically speaking, would never have been elected. However, I believe that God, in His ultimate wisdom and mercy, put them into that position for a reason. And these men followed through on it.

Everyone has a free will and presidents can choose to do what is right or not, but these significant men we are going to study changed the relationship between our nation and Israel. Once we became a blessing to Israel, God blessed our nation. That is the key. More than 3,000 years ago, God revealed Himself to Abraham and said, "I've got something for you, Abe, that you are not going to believe; this is such a deal!"

"I will make you into a great nation, and I will bless you; I will make your name great, and you will be a blessing. I will bless those who bless you, and whoever curses you I will curse; and all peoples on earth will be blessed through you." Gen. 12:2-3 NIV

God made an unusual and unconditional covenant with Abraham - there were no conditions. It doesn't matter who you are, no matter what you believe, if you are a blessing to Abraham's descendants, God is going to bless you.

God will bless those who bless Abraham's descendants and, remember, those descendants are the Jewish people.

This certainly has not been the history of what's going on in the world. The Lord God MUST bless, because he promised to do so and He is not going to weasel out of these promises.

Especially during the last ten years, God has proven this over and over again. The focus of my Christian walk has been looking at these elements: **how have nations treated Israel and what has been the outcome for those nations?**

At some point in history, almost all the nations have turned against the Jews. I pray that our nation never will do that, but if we do, we will know what the consequences are going to be.

God will bless you, as an individual, and us as a community, because He promised that He will bless the nation that is a blessing to Abraham's descendants - the Jewish nation and especially the People, the nation of Israel today.

God WILL and He MUST bless you if you bless the Children of Israel!

So now, join me, as we are going to look at some of these people that God pulled out of nowhere and selected them to be His INSTRUMENTS.

John Somerville

Spring 2020

PART 1

HARRY S. TRUMAN

HARRY S. TRUMAN 1884 – 1972

Harry S. Truman (May 8, 1884 – December 26, 1972) was the 33rd president of the United States from 1945 to 1953, succeeding upon the death of Franklin D. Roosevelt after serving as vice president. His implementation of the Marshall Plan helped rebuild Western Europe's postwar economy. He established the Truman Doctrine and NATO.

During the 1948 presidential elections he won a surprise victory that secured his own presidential term. Truman oversaw the Berlin Airlift of 1948 and gained United Nations approval for what later became known as the Korean War. His 1948 Executive Orders started racial integration in the military and federal agencies. Truman is ranked as one of the best presidents.

Harry S. Truman was born in Lamar, Missouri, on May 8, 1884, the oldest child of John Anderson Truman and Martha Ellen Young Truman.
He was named after his maternal uncle and his middle initial "S" honors his grandfathers. Little Harry's siblings were John Vivian and Mary Jane.

Their father was a good man who worked as a farmer and horse trader with a knack for losing money and opportunities. They settled for a while at Martha's father's farm near Grandview, Missouri. It was a wonderful 600-acre (240 ha) farm where John spent much of his working life as did Harry's brother, Vivian. For about ten years, Harry farmed at his grandfather's Grandview until the United States entered the Great War (WWI) in 1917.

Because Little Harry was suffering from bad eyesight, he had to wear glasses from an early age. Forbidden to play rough games because of the expensive glasses, Harry became a 'mama's boy'. He learned to play the piano - not something farm boys did in those days. Harry became such a good musician that he even considered a career as a concert pianist. Besides reading the Bible, he loved military history books and dreamed of going to West Point or the Naval Academy.

Realizing Harry was a bright child, his parents decided to temporarily move to the city while the grandparents continued to run the farm. Harry was enrolled in a good public school in Independence, Missouri.
His first grade teacher in 1893, Miss Mira Ewin, remembered her famous pupil. "I never had to reprimand him a single time," she said in a 1947 interview. "He just smiled his way along. [He] was a very studious boy. When other boys were out playing ball, he was reading."

8

One of Harry's classmates admired the fact that he was always studious. As God would lead them, their new home in Independence happened to be next door to an Orthodox Jewish family. In an interview, Sarah Viner (the daughter of that family) said, "Oh yes, little Harry! He came to our house all the time; he and my brother Abe were friends. Harry became so close to us that for years, he served as our 'Shabbas Goy'.

A **Shabbos goy** is a non-Jew who performs certain types of work which Jewish religious law does not permit the Jew to do on the Sabbath. 'Shabbos' means the Sabbath; 'goy' literally means "a nation" but colloquially means a "non-Jew."

The Jewish seed that was planted in that little boy's heart was not stomped on by his parents. They certainly gave him permission to perform those acts of kindness. Independence, at the turn of the century, still had the characteristics of a Civil War frontier border town. It was a time when racial prejudices and anti-Semitism were part and parcel of everyday conversation. Despite the fact there were very few Jews in the area, (the ones that lived there were an oddity) most locals were wary of foreigners, unusual foods and religions. Evidently, Harry's parents never told him, "Harry! Don't go over to those Jews next-door! Smell that food, that smells bad. Just stay away from them." Instead, his mother permitted the six-year old boy to go there. This encouragement made it possible for the seed to sprout and grow, which eventually not only blessed our nation but the Jewish nation as well.

During high school, for English class Harry wrote an insightful essay about Shylock the Jew in Shakespeare's Merchant of Venice. He could have expressed the general attitudes prevalent during that time such as: "Shylock was just another Jew who was only out to get money." Uncharacteristically for that time, his essay didn't contain a negative word about the Jews but showed his honest, predisposed concern for the Jewish people.

The following review of the essay shows how much of Truman's character and personality were already developed in the 14-year-old teenager.

"Harry doesn't bother with much of the plot at all when he writes about Shylock. Instead he criticizes Christians for not following their beliefs, for not loving their enemies as they say they should do. Who, he asks, "instituted . . . that very Christian institution, the Inquisition? Now if the Christians carry not out their teachings, who's to carry them out? Not China, nor Turkey and surely not the Jews." Harry is sympathetic to Shylock and feels he could not have done anything differently than he did in the play. "Think of him leaving the court room, broken, childless, everything but killed. He said he was content to die. What else could he do?" Shylock sought to revenge himself on the people who hurt him. Harry understands this completely. "I never saw a Jew, Christian or any other man who, if he had the chance, wouldn't take revenge, although he may say 'Love your enemies' and a lot of other things of the same sort."

Raymond H. Geselbracht, author of *The Boy Who Would be President* and Special Assistant to the Director at the Harry S. Truman Library, writes,

"It is truly amazing to read the teenager's words and to listen to recordings of the retired president back in Independence and to marvel at how similar they sound. I don't believe anyone ever had to say to him, "Harry why don't you grow up." It seems that he was always a 'grown-up' who just happened to get older."

Harry Truman was the last president of the USA who never went to or

graduated from a college. Despite (or perhaps because of) that, he became one of our most respected and down-to-earth presidents.

Upon finishing high school in 1901, Harry moved to Kansas City where he attended a business school for a year and then worked in a variety of clerical jobs in a bank and on the railroad.

Harry 1901

His bad eyesight prevented Harry from being admitted to West Point, so instead, he joined the Missouri National Guard and eventually passed the eye exam by memorizing the chart.

The blue National Guard uniform resembled the Federal Army ('Damn Yankee') Civil War uniform. One day, Harry visited his parents who had moved back to the Grandview farm.

Upon seeing Harry wearing that uniform, his elderly grandmother, an un-reconstructed Southerner, almost had a stroke. He would never wear the uniform in her presence again. After serving in the National Guard from 1905 to 1911, Harry 'retired' as a Corporal and hung up the blue uniform - out of Granny's sight, of course.

Meeting the Jacobson family

David and Sarah Jacobson were impoverished Jewish immigrants from Lithuania. Their son Eddie was born in 1891 in New York's Lower East Side. Not wanting their children to grow up in the tenements and streets of New York, the father decided to move his family to Leavenworth, Kansas. Eventually they settled down in Kansas City, Missouri in 1905.

Harry and Eddie became acquainted when Eddie was employed in the haberdashery business in Kansas City. Each day, the seasoned 14-year-old teenager took the daily deposits to the bank where the 21-year-old Harry worked as a clerk. Upon his grandfather's death, Harry was called back to the farm because his father needed all the help he could muster.

For the next 11 years, Harry was looking at the south end of a team of horses plowing North, not because he loved it, but because he had to.

However, he continued to harbor those daring dreams of war and gallantry he read about all his life.

The following story is about the relationship of a Gentile Christian future president and a Reform Jew. God used their friendship in a miraculous way.

In 1916 and 1917, the First World War was still raging in Europe and it seemed that the USA might get involved as well. Rejoining the Missouri National Guard, Harry was promoted to lieutenant. One member of his unit was a Jewish private named Eddie Jacobson. More than 11 years had passed since they had last seen each other, but when Eddie met his commanding officer it immediately 'clicked'. Their artillery unit, Battery D, 129th Field Artillery of the 35th Division, was sent to Oklahoma to practice their combat firing skills.

Private Eddie

Lt. Harry

12

While being stationed in this desert encampment, Harry suggested to Eddie, "Why don't we start a canteen? We'll sell coffee, pop and doughnuts, and from the money we make we can buy baseball and football gear for our troops."

Truman's diary and the letters he wrote to his girlfriend Bess back in Independence mention the fact that the two men began working together, "Eddie Jacobson is a cracker-jack and he is a Jew!"

They made some money, went to war together and carried out their duties under fire extremely well. The bond between the two friends deepened. In 1918, the victorious and surviving soldiers returned to the USA and were demobilized.

As Eddie didn't have a job and Harry didn't want to go back to the farm, they decided to open a business together. "I know haberdashery, shirts and ties, collars and hats," Eddie said.

The two friends borrowed money and opened a store in downtown Kansas City, across the street from the Muehlebach Hotel. The shop became a popular place for the boys from 'Battery D' to hang out and occasionally buy things, while those visiting the best hotel in Kansas City created a nice flow of patrons.

Things were looking good - until the economic crash of 1921.

Harry and Eddie's business was forced to close. Usually, when a company goes bankrupt, the partners blame each other, often ending in lawsuits. However, this is not what happened with Truman and Jacobson.

Imagine what the people in Harry's Baptist church may have said to him, "Harry, we told you so! You were unequally yoked with that Jew. Why did you go into business with that Jew? It was probably all his fault and I'll bet he robbed you somehow. You know how those Jews are about money." Truman would not listen to them.

Trying to get out of debt, Jacobson was forced to go back on the road, knocking on doors and selling shirts.

Tom Pendergast

Jim Pendergast, a nephew of a crooked Kansas City politician named Tom Pendergast, also happened to have been in Harry's outfit fighting in France.

"Why don't you go into politics? Jim suggested to Harry. "You no longer have a store. Why don't you run for the eastern county judge? My uncle Tom is the head of the county Democrat party; he'll make sure you win the election."

Because Harry never went to college or law school, his job description was to run the county, not to act as a legal judge.

My Platform

Good Roads

A Budgeted Road Fund

Economy

A Day's Work For a Day's Pay

Fewer Automobiles and More Work for County Employees

Harry S. Truman

1922

New Road and Precinct Map Showing WHERE TO VOTE FOR

Harry S. Truman
Democratic Candidate For
JUDGE, EASTERN DISTRICT
Jackson County

It was the beginning of Harry's incredible and improbable political career. The friendship between the fledgling politician and the traveling salesman continued and through the years, the Jew and the Gentile always stayed in touch.

In 1919 the newlyweds, Truman and Bess moved into the big house on North Delaware in Independence. Ruling the roost was his mother-in-law, Madge Gates Wallace. Her first house rule was, "There will never be a Jew in this house!"

True to her word, for as long as they lived, Harry's good friend Eddie never entered that home. Not only was Mrs. Wallace an outspoken anti-Semite, she despised her son-in-law and always reminded him that he was just a dirt farmer and a failed businessman.

When the Truman family moved to DC, old Madge went right along with them and even had her own room in the White House.

For 33 years, the 'failure' and no account dirt farmer who wasn't good enough for her daughter, looked after her.

After Madge died, Bess continued to enforce her mother's policy about Jews not being allowed to enter her house. Bess never found out about the secret Sunday morning kitchen meeting the retired president had with some Israeli Jews who called him to say hello when they happened to pass through town. Truman invited them over but warned them that it would be a short meeting because Bess was at her church service and would be back before noon.

I hope Bess doesn't read this 'Top Secret' information. (Since no one has heard from her since 1982, I don't think there is much chance of that. Bess holds the record of the longest-lived First Lady and longest-lived Second Lady. She died in 1982, at the age of 97.)

Today, not only Jews, but Eskimos and Martians can walk through her house because it belongs to the National Park Service and is open to the public.

Whenever Harry was back in town, he often had dinner at Eddie's house, played poker and sipped some Wild Turkey with his card-playing pals.

Always staying in touch, these two friends grew old together. When Truman became president, only one man was allowed to walk into his office at any time - his Jewish pal, Eddie Jacobson.

Calling himself a 'light-foot Baptist', Harry meant that he didn't hold to the strict Baptist beliefs about no dancing and card playing. Truman wrote, "I am a Baptist because I think that this sect gives the common man the shortest and most direct approach to God."
Even though Eddie had been raised in the Jewish Orthodox tradition, he became less concerned about the religious tenets of his Jewishness and joined the B'nai B'rith and a Reform Temple in Kansas City.

After serving a couple of terms as county judge, Harry was elected senator in 1935. No one in Jackson County suspected that one day, Harry would become vice president under Franklin Roosevelt. The

man who became president four times (1932-1944) was in the habit of changing vice presidents like he was changing his socks.
In this picture, FDR's 1st vice president John Nance 'Cactus Jack' Garner whips out a couple of Jessie James' pistols to show off to the rookie Senator.

The United States was forced into WW II following the attack at Pearl Harbor in December 1941.
Even General Eisenhower, the Supreme Commander of the Allied Forces in Europe, didn't know about the atrocities behind the lines. Many rabbis and most of their Brooklyn congregants who immigrated from eastern Europe received postcards from family members still in Europe, saying, "We are being relocated to the East. Everything will be fine. When we get there, I will write again."
In millions of cases that postcard was the last news they would ever hear from their family members.

Anti-Jewish measures began when Hitler came to power in 1933 and now, we know that by the early 40s, hundreds of thousands of Jews were systematically being murdered. Even though by October 1943, at least two million Jews already had been murdered by the Nazis, hardly anyone knew for certain about the unspeakable crimes being committed.

On October 6, 1943, 300 rabbis came to Washington DC, with the understanding that they would meet with the president. In the eyes of most of the Jewish community FDR was a great hero, and they revered him. Determined to meet with the president, the rabbis rehearsed the following message,

"Mister President, we've gotten word and proof from hundreds of our brethren that the Nazis are taking them into these camps and killing the Jews by the hundreds of thousands. Please sir, direct our Army Air Corps to stop bombing the German factories for just a couple of days and bomb the railway lines going into a killing factory called Auschwitz in eastern Poland or bomb that death factory in Auschwitz, because now we know for certain they are killing all the Jews sent there."

Rabbis gathering at the Lincoln Memorial before their march to White House.

 Roosevelt, who was a politician through and through, knew that there weren't many votes in that Orthodox community and there wasn't much they could do for him. Because he already wrapped up the Jewish vote in NY, he didn't need this small and impoverished group to vote for him. When the president was told that the 'March of the Rabbis' was on the way to the White House he responded, "I don't have time for this." (His diary shows that nothing was scheduled for that day.)

"March of the Rabbis"

Deeming this meeting a worthless and pointless political event which had no pay off for him, he determined to get out of the building.

"Find me something to do, quick!" he ordered and rolled out the back door. His chauffeur drove him to a local air force base where a sergeant major was celebrating a promotion or retirement. The president had his excuse.

The group of rabbis were intercepted outside the White House and told, "Sorry, Rabbis, no one is at home. The president has been called away on something vitally important. Just give us a paper outlining your concerns. Tell him what he can do for you and I assure you that he will give it his undivided attention as soon as he returns."

And thus, the Bergson Group rabbis were turned away at a crucial moment in time. If the president had taken the time to listen to them, he might have saved three or four million lives! He could have given the order to bomb Auschwitz, but he was indifferent to their pleas.

The *New York Times*, 7 October 1943.

A tiny article, buried in the *NY Times* read, "Grand Rabbi Horowitz at this gathering, sang prayers for the Jewish dead, prayed for the president, for the US government and for victory in the war. All sang the National Anthem in Hebrew."

Look closely at the picture and see if these men were joined by Church representatives.

Do you recognize Christian leaders who were joined this Jewish group on their march to the White House and were turned away?

On that day, NO Christian leaders marched arm in arm to the White House.

We can't find ANY Christian or Catholic leaders, nor any big-time evangelists that stood with them that day.

I am certain that, had one or two Bishops or a Cardinal been with these rabbis, they would have been welcomed to tell their story to the president. That is what politics is all about.

> **Proverbs 24:11**
> *"Rescue those being led away to death; hold back those staggering towards slaughter. If you say, "But we knew nothing about this", does not He who weighs the heart perceive it? Does not He who guards your life know it? Will He not repay everyone according to what they have done?"*

These verses mean so much to me because it is God's Word. We can't close our eyes to these kinds of things, like the Christian leaders did back in 1943. The Jews stood there, all alone on those steps and were turned away. That was not a blessing to Abraham's descendants. The church was silent in 1933 and 1943 and in…. you fill in the details.

After having served two terms as vice president , President Roosevelt wanted to get rid of Jack Garner.
"How do you sum up your time as vice president ?" a reporter asked him.
"It ain't worth a bucket of warm spit," Garner responded, of course meaning something else. He hated the VP job because it was a 'nothing' job.

Henry Wallace and Roosevelt

The new vice president picked by Roosevelt, Henry Wallace, turned out to be some kind of liberal wacko. While running for the 4th time, Roosevelt decided to get rid of Wallace as well.
He went through the list of potential VPs, but everyone had something that would hurt him one way or another.

20

Finally, one of his advisors suggested, "What about Harry Truman?"

"Who?"

"That Senator from Pendergast. You know... that dirt farmer from Missouri."

"Does he have any baggage?" FDR asked.

"No sir, he's straight and squeaky clean like an arrow. "

"Sounds alright to me. Are there any other problems with him?"

The real problem was that Harry didn't want the job under any circumstances!

The next Democratic convention was to be held in Chicago and because it was the 4th presidential run for Roosevelt, he didn't even bother to attend. He knew that the nomination was just a formality. He was a shoe-in. However, because the Constitution demanded it, Roosevelt needed to add a vice president to the ticket. He didn't really care who it was because the past 12 years had proven to him that he didn't really need an understudy. To him, having a vice president was just a legal necessity, so he hardly ever met with any of them nor had them prepared to take over. When asked about his interest in filling the VP slot, Truman routinely responded with, "No, no, no! The vice president simply presides over the Senate and sits around hoping for a funeral." (He was probably thinking that former VP Cactus Jack Garner was right about 'that bucket of spit.')

Robert (Bob) Hannegan, the incoming Democratic National Chairman, informed FDR that Truman was not interested in the job. Because the Chicago convention was about to begin, and time was running out, FDR and Hannegan cooked up a scheme to trick Truman into accepting the post.

They scripted a scenario for a phone call that would blame Truman for losing the election and possibly even the war if he didn't get on board. That phone call was staged to be 'accidentally' overheard by Truman.

Senator Truman was summoned to the seventh-floor suite of Chicago's Blackstone Hotel. The room was jammed with Democratic party bosses who had been ordered to jump on the reluctant nominee after the phone call came in from the president who was in his train on the West Coast.

Roosevelt didn't talk on the phone but habitually bellowed so loudly that the listener was in danger of damaging his eardrum. Automatically, the listener held the receiver far away from his ear, which of course allowed everyone else in the room to clearly overhear what the President was saying.

As Truman sat on the edge of a bed in the smoke-filled and overcrowded hotel room, the president yelled, "Bob, what about that Senator from Missouri? You got him lined up yet to be the VP?"

"No sir, he's the orneriest Missouri mule I've ever run into. He doesn't want to be VP."

Roosevelt continued with his pre-planned tirade, "Well, you just tell him, that if he wants to split the Democratic party right in the middle of a war and we end up losing this election and this war, it's all on his head." FDR dramatically slammed the phone down.

Not knowing about the setup, the stunned Truman thought Roosevelt really meant what he said. *Why didn't he tell me that directly?* he wondered. Turning to the others in the room, he said, "Boys, if it's really true that we could lose everything... I don't have a choice. Okay, you can nominate me tonight."

The trick worked. Truman campaigned hard and got both himself and Roosevelt elected.

However, during the four months of the campaign and the first 82 days of the 4th Roosevelt Administration, Truman hardly ever saw the President in person and had little idea of what was going on.

When the President did invite him to the White House, Truman expected to be briefed about the war aims and the plans for the upcoming end of the war.

The invitation turned out to be just a public relations breakfast, and it is not clear if they even ate.

The photographers took the necessary pictures of the President and the new vice president , and that was it - Roosevelt told Truman nothing.

After Inauguration Day, January 20, 1945, the new vice president would have only two meetings alone with Roosevelt. Truman said he hated both meetings. "He does all the talking and he talks about what he wants to talk about, and he never talks about anything you want to talk about, so there isn't much you can do."

The Yalta Conference was held in Yalta, Crimea during February 1945. Heads of the governments of the United States, the United Kingdom and the Soviet Union discussed Europe's postwar reorganization. The Yalta conference had been preceded by the Tehran Conference in 1943, and followed by the Potsdam Conference in July 1945, which was attended by Stalin, Churchill and Harry S. Truman.

Top: Yalta Conference, February 1945
Right: Potsdam Conference, July 1945

FDR and King Ibn Saud meeting

After the Yalta Conference, FDR (who would die two months later) met with King Ibn Saud of Saudi Arabia in the Great Bitter Lake of the Suez Canal on Valentine's Day of 1945 aboard a US Navy vessel, the U.S.S. *Quincy.*

Roosevelt believed that by his personal diplomacy he could easily persuade Saud into approving at least 10,000 Jewish refugees to immigrate into Palestine by the dint of his charm and personality.

FDR gave the king a DC-3 passenger plane, which marked the beginning of the Saudi Air Force. When he saw that the king had trouble walking, FDR spontaneously gave him one of his own wheelchairs.

The president asked for a map that showed how small Palestine was compared to all the Arab lands, hoping that the comparison would somehow sway the king into acquiescing. He then tried to persuade by appealing to the king's compassion (which didn't exist) by pointing out there was no other place in the world where this tiny number of pitiful survivors could go except Palestine.

Colonel William A. Eddie USMC (ret.), the State Department's U.S. Minister to Saudi Arabia, translated the meeting. Col. Eddie who was fluent in both Arabic and 'Marinecorpseze' (as well as English) described FDR's presentation,

"President Roosevelt was in top form as a charming host, witty conversationalist, with the spark and light in his eyes and that gracious smile which always won people over to him whenever he talked with them as a friend. . . . With Ibn Saud he was at his very best."

That day however, "his very best" wasn't good enough.

"Absolutely not!" the King exclaimed angrily. "Not one Jew is going to enter into Palestine. It's unfair. It's not our fault that they were killed in Europe."

He was adamant and closed the discussion with his final statement on the subject, "The Arabs rather would choose to die, than yield their land to the Jews."

To which Roosevelt responded, "You know, Your Highness, I learned more about the Arab culture in five minutes with you than all my advisors ever taught me."

> Due to the continued US involvement in World War II, relations with Saudi Arabia were put on the 'back burner'. As the war progressed, the United States more fully understood that Saudi oil was of strategic importance. In 1943, FDR had declared that "the defense of Saudi Arabia is vital to the defense of the United States". As a result of the talks with Ibn Saud, the US gained permission for military aircraft heading to Iran and the Soviet Union to use Saudi airspace. In 1944 the first American consulate had opened in Dhahran.

One of the last things President Roosevelt did in his life was to write a final letter about the Palestine question to the King of Arabia. (See next page)

April 5, 1945

His Majesty
ABDUL AZIZ IBN ABDUR RAHMAN AL FAISAL AL SAUD
King of Saudi Arabia, Riyadh

GREAT AND GOOD FRIEND:

I have received the communication which Your Majesty sent me under date of March 10, 1945, in which you refer to the question of Palestine and to the continuing interest of the Arabs in current developments affecting that country.

I am gratified that Your Majesty took this occasion to bring your views on this question to my attention and I have given the most careful attention to the statements which you make in your letter. I am also mindful of the memorable conversation which we had not so long ago and in the course of which I had an opportunity to obtain so vivid an impression of Your Majesty's sentiments on this question.

Your Majesty will recall that on previous occasions I communicated to you the attitude of the American Government toward Palestine and made clear our desire that no decision be taken with respect to the basic situation in that country without full consultation with both Arabs and Jews. Your Majesty will also doubtless recall that during our recent conversation I assured you that I would take no action, in my capacity as Chief of the Executive Branch of this Government, which might prove hostile to the Arab people.

It gives me pleasure to renew to Your Majesty the assurances which you have previously received regarding the attitude of my Government and my own, as Chief Executive, with regard to the question of Palestine and to inform you that the policy of this Government in this respect is unchanged.

I desire also at this time to send you my best wishes for Your Majesty's continued good health and for the welfare of your people.

Your Good Friend,

FRANKLIN D. ROOSEVELT

The president assured the king the USA would take no action that could prove hostile to the Arab people. First there would be consultations (even though he already knew the Arab response, "No Jews allowed into Palestine") before any Jews would enter Palestine. After the war, he promised, no Jews would come into the land.

One week after the letter to King Ibn Saud was written, America and the world were shocked by the sudden death of FDR.

"Truman is the Nation's Chief", one of the newspaper headlines read. Because FDR had changed vice presidents three times, most people didn't even know who Truman was.

That afternoon of 12 April 1945, when Truman was summoned to the White House, he was unaware that the president had died.
Mrs. Roosevelt approached him and said, "The president is dead."
The first thing Truman said was, "Mrs. Roosevelt, what can I do for you?"
"It's not what you can do for me, what can we do for you? For you are the one in trouble now!" was her answer.

After serving as vice president for only 82 days, Truman had to be quickly sworn in as president.
Truman's wife Bess and their daughter Margaret were quickly located and brought to the White House, while a frantic search ensued for a Bible on which to swear in the 33rd President of the United States. Finally, after a long search, a Gideon Bible was located and dusted off for the ceremony.

The Truman family was surrounded by Roosevelt's Cabinet members, totally dedicated to Roosevelt, whom they had expected to serve for life. FDR had been an aristocratic figure, while Truman was looked upon as a hick farmer and a county courthouse hack.

"How can he possibly dare to sit on the grand throne of FDR?" groused many of the White House staff.

In this picture the people not only looked shocked, because their heroic president just died, but there is also a look of disdain.

During the initial months and years of his terms, Harry Truman had to contend with this continued disdain and lack of respect.

When Truman left his home the next morning, a mob of reporters was waiting for him on the sidewalk. The initial shock began to wear off and the reality of the awesome task ahead was coming into focus.

He told the reporters, "Boys, I don't know how many of you are praying people, but you've got to pray for me now. I don't know how many of you ever have had a load of hay drop on your head. Well, right now I just feel like the sun and the moon and the stars all fell right on top of me. I need your prayers!"

> ## Truman Diary, entry June 17, 1945
>
> *I have to decide Japanese strategy - shall we invade Japan proper or shall we bomb and blockade? That is my hardest decision to date. But I'll make it when I have all the facts.*

Truman had been just informed about the invasion plan of Japan and the atomic bomb being tested. He was totally unprepared to take over as president let alone as a War Time Leader. There was an immense backlog of Top-Secret information as well as presidential decisions that had to be quickly made. Briefings and papers had to be intensely studied, devoured and understood.

The day Truman entered office, a stack of State Department memos counseled him that the Balfour Declaration pledge should be abandoned—and that if the Jews persisted in their suicidal intention to declare statehood, they should be left to face the consequences.

Thankfully, he had a no-nonsense focused mind bolstered by years of inquisitive reading and investigation. He was quoted as saying,

"Not all readers are leaders, but all leaders are readers."

Indeed, he was a fast reader, good listener and a quick learner capable of grasping most complicated situations quickly.

When the Second World War ended and the fullness of the horrific murder of Jews and others in Europe by the Nazis became known, Truman was appalled. We now know that even more than six million Jews were murdered.

Europe was divided among the British, Russians, Americans and French and most of the information about the death camps came from the American sector. General Eisenhower insisted that army photographers took pictures of everything in the concentration camps, to be recorded for posterity. Even before grasping the enormity of the slaughter, he said, "Someday, some S.O.B. is going to say this never happened. I want to document the truth now, before the evidence disappears."

> **Dwight David "Ike" Eisenhower** (1890 – 1969) was an American Army general and 34th President of the United States (1953 -1961). During World War II, he was a five-star general in the United States Army and served as Supreme Commander of the Allied Expeditionary Forces in Europe. He planned and supervised the invasion of North Africa in 1942–43 and the successful invasion of France and Germany in 1944–45 from the Western Front.

Eisenhower and Truman

Much of the horrific evidence from the other European sectors was not meticulously recorded.

Without that undeniable record of photographs and films, the Holocaust would just be a written record easily dismissed.

Eisenhower's pictures have endured as warnings to the world that it could easily happen again. Seeing the unedited pictures, Truman was sickened and stunned. As was his style of thinking, he immediately asked what could be done for the survivors? In the British sector, British troops kept many Jewish survivors in the very same concentration camps in which the Nazis had imprisoned them. The majority of the survivors no longer had a family or a home or even a village to return to. An entire region and a way of life had been destroyed.

When interviewed, most of the survivors stated emphatically that they wanted to go to Palestine, because it was believed to be the only place of refuge on the planet for them.

However, the British were keeping these Jews as prisoners so that they couldn't go to the homeland they had been promised by that same government 28 years before by the Balfour Declaration of 1917.

When Truman learned about this incarceration, he demanded that Britain release 100,000 of these survivors from Displaced Persons (DP) camps and allow them to immediately immigrate to Palestine, which was still part of the British Mandate.

During WWII, as Britain's main ally, the USA had assisted and saved Britain's bacon many times. After the war ended, the United States continued to help rebuild and feed the Brits, and Germans and other Europeans. Truman told Britain, "Get the Jews out of those horrible camps. There is room for them in Palestine!"

However, the newly elected British Labour government adamantly refused to allow any of those Jews to leave for Palestine. Their Foreign Secretary, **Ernest Bevin,** even re-phrased Truman's demand for 100,000 Jews to be released to mean that the US wanted many Jews to leave New York City.

This refusal to help the most helpless of Abraham's descendants was one of the root causes for the disintegration of the British Empire. Long ago, God had promised to curse those who cursed His Chosen People. This treatment of the Jews was just one of many worsening 'curses' instigated by the British Government that caused the British Empire to fall.

Bevin

YEAR: 1950

31

Harry and Eddie

Truman continued to stay in touch with his old Army buddy and former business partner, Eddie Jacobson.

After fifteen long years, by 1947 both Harry and Eddie had paid off their haberdashery failure debts.

That same year, the British government told the UN they wanted out of their Palestinian Mandate - they were washing their hands of the whole mess. The UN attempted to tackle the problem by coming up with a partition plan that was patterned on the Solomonic solution of cutting the baby in two, forgetting that Solomon never had to do the division.

Truman had been stumped in his efforts to work out a plan for a peaceful settlement among the Jews and the Arabs in solving the Palestine question. At first, Truman was all for the Partition Plan, where the remaining parts of the British Mandate were to be divided between an Arab and Jewish state. The idea seemed reasonable and right to him.

However, the Partition Plan caused a lot of national confusion and unrest. For a variety of reasons, many American Jews didn't think the State of Israel should come into being. Others said, "Yes, it must be done. It's the only place in the world where Jews can be free."

After meeting with all sides, Truman's diary entry read:

"The Arabs, I cannot even talk to them. There is no compromising on their part. They won't give an inch, and some of the American Jews are just as bad, they don't like this idea of a Jewish state because they are afraid they will have to move there or be accused of divided loyalty."

Other American Jews wanted it so badly they forgot how to behave. Jumping up in the president's office, one Rabbi slammed his hand on the president's desk, demanding, "You've got to do it right now!"

"Can you imagine this rabbi shouting at the president of the USA and telling him what he must do?" Truman wrote.

He noticed that immediately after leaving his office, each group shared their personal interpretation of the meeting with the press. Of course, they had a field day, causing Truman's public approval ratings to take a nosedive.

During the 1948 elections Truman wanted to be elected on his own, but his approval ratings were going down all the time. The Arab/Israel issue was like a "third rail" which shocks or electrocutes anyone touching it. When the issue reached a boiling point, in exasperation he said, "That's it! I don't want to hear any more about it. We'll turn the problem over to the UN and let them sort it out. That's what we invented the UN for anyhow."

This 'washing his hands of the problem' behavior was unlike Truman's farmer mentality which always seemed to find a way to fix any problem that arose in the field. The fact that he seemed to have given up and turned it over to a bunch of diplomats (for which he had no use or respect) speaks volumes about his frustration.

At the same time, some Zionist leaders in New York City knew they had to talk to the president to see if they could change his mind. The stubborn Missouri mule in the President kicked up his hooves - adamantly he refused to see anyone regarding the Palestine question.

Scratching their heads, the New York Zionists wondered how they could break through Truman's iron curtain.

Suddenly one of them had an idea.

Truman with Missouri Mules

33

"What about that *shmatta* guy in Kansas City?" one of them suggested. "I was just at a Bnai Brith meeting out in KC where they gave that clothing guy an award. I can't remember his name, but he's a bald, old pal of Harry Truman."

Pooling all their coins, they started making calls from a pay phone.

"Can you connect me to a Mr. Jacobstein?" the caller asked the Kansas City operator. Then they tried a Mr. Jacoby, or other variations of that name. Over and over, the only response they got from calling those Kansas City numbers was someone yelling, "I don't know what you're talking about!" and slamming down the receiver.

Late that evening, they got in touch with a man named A.J. Granoff, a Jewish lawyer. "Do you know someone called Jacobstein, who is a friend of Harry Truman?"

"You mean Eddie Jacobson? Of course I know him. I happen to be his lawyer and a good friend."

"We have to talk to him right away."

When Eddie picked up the phone, the man on the line from New York City told him, "Eddie, you've got to do us the biggest favor for the future State of Israel. You have to go and see Harry Truman, and ask him to...."

"Hold it right there!" Eddie cut in. "I have never used my friendship with the president to ask him for anything and I'm not going to do it for ... whoever you are."

"Whoa, wait a minute, Mr. Jacobson! This is a matter of life and death for our Jewish brothers and sisters and children in Palestine who are fighting for their lives. The president needs to understand the dire straits they are in."

"Harry Truman will do what is right when he knows all the facts."

"Listen Eddie that's just the point. We've got to get him the facts face to face."

"I'm not a Zionist," Eddie interrupted him. "I don't know the first thing to tell him about Palestine and what's going on there. If you want me to talk to the president, I'm not going to ask him for a favor. However, if I'm going to present him with facts, then you better spin me up pretty quick on those facts."

"Well, Eddie, hop on an airplane to New York as soon as you can. Time is of the essence. If you're the bright guy we think you are, we'll teach you everything you need to know as quickly as you can absorb it.

When can you get here?"

"OK. I'll be flying east as soon as I can get a ticket and find someone to mind the store," Eddie promised. "I've got my own store now. Did I tell you I was back in the clothing business, like when Harry and I started out after the war?"

At the same time Eddie tried to organize a flight to the east coast, from the other side of the world a man was heading west to New York. Even though neither had ever heard of the other, these two men would be forever linked to the history of Israel.

> **Chaim Azriel Weizmann** (1874 –1952) a Zionist leader, president of the Zionist Organization and future first president of Israel. Born in Belarus, after finishing high school Weizman earned a doctorate in Chemistry in Switzerland. While living in England, he developed a new synthetic acetone which was used during WW I and II. Weizman became well known and respected by Churchill, David Lloyd-George and Arthur Balfour.

God elevated **Chaim Weizmann** for His own purposes, just as He was doing with Harry and Eddie. They all played their disparate parts in the grand tapestry of His plan.

Weizmann's bearing, self-assurance and mastery of the issues made people think that he spoke for millions of Jews, but the fact is that he hardly had any followers at all.

Standing firm in what he believed in, Weizmann eventually picked up the mantle and aura of the deceased Theodore Herzl to promote a moderate "Practical Zionism".

His willingness to compromise earned him the undying enmity of Zionist hard-liners like David Ben-Gurion, the future first prime minister of Israel. That is the reason why you don't find Weizmann's signature on the Israeli Declaration of Independence - Ben-Gurion wouldn't allow it.

The 74 year old Chaim Weizmann, who was growing blind and in failing health, arrived in New York on February 4, 1948. His hope of getting just one more chance to meet with the president before the UN would slam the door on the Israeli hope for a state of their own, was growing dim. Three months earlier, he met with the president, who now felt that he knew everything that Weizmann could tell him. Although admiring the elderly scientist, Truman feared that if he opened the door to the Oval Office just a crack for him, if it became known, he would have to let everyone in all over again. Not about to fall for that trick, Harry was also hesitant to come under the spell of such a passionate and persuasive personality.

Truman was exhausted and frustrated by the myriad of positions that the Palestine question encompassed. It was already hard enough trying to handle the Palestine problem over the past three years and ending up making the weakest of decisions to turn it over to the UN. But if he let Weizmann get close... he might have to change his mind again.
Truman prided himself on making the "Buck stops here" decisions and then go to bed and forget about it.

"It is understanding that gives us an ability to have peace. When we understand the other fellow's viewpoint, and he understands our, then we can sit down and work out our differences. The buck stops here."

~Harry S. Truman
1884-1972
33rd President of the United States

The moment Truman did relent and let Weizmann in , things began to change in heaven and on earth.

Chaim Weizman played a key role in the creation of the State of Israel, but it was Eddie Jacobson who managed to get the tightly shut Oval Office door pried open. It took some old country Jewish *chutzpah*.

After attempting to reach President Truman by letter and getting a delayed and unsatisfactory response, Eddie decided to take a more aggressive approach. He feared that time was running out and knew that Harry didn't sense the urgency. That was when Eddie decided that he must talk turkey to his friend .

That Saturday morning, March 13, Eddie arrived at the White House without an appointment or an invitation.

Before he could enter the Oval Office, he was intercepted by Matt Connelly, the Appointments Secretary.

"Mr. Jacobson, I can guess why you are here," he began. "But please, I beg of you, don't talk about Palestine to the president. His blood pressure will shoot through the roof. He doesn't want to hear about it. He has shut the door on any more discussions about the subject. Don't do it," he pleaded. "I beg of you. If the boss is upset... we're all upset."

Eddie may have been thinking, *I've flown all the way here from Kansas City and paid my own way for one purpose and I almost feel that I could be on a mission from God* as he briskly walked into the presidential office.

Truman, working at his desk, was pleasantly surprised to see his friend so unexpectedly. Even though the meeting was not recorded, we know what happened in that office from Eddie Jacobson's handwritten notes which he jotted down right after that meeting.

"Eddie! It's so good to see you!" Truman exclaimed. "How are things back home? Does it look like a late Spring? Can the farmers get into the fields? Tell me, how's Bluma and the girls? Listen Eddie, I gotta tell you, this city is the worst back-stabbing, double-crossing place in the world." Truman ranted and raved on, "No matter what I do, somehow it gets turned around and some reporter or bureaucrat will stab me in the back. It's really difficult. Bess and I had to go down to Key West for a week just to get out of this lousy town. I'd give anything to get back home to Missouri. Hey, maybe we could reopen our haberdashery again and this time make a go of it."

The conversation sounded like they were sitting at the poker table in Eddie's basement. It was just like old times – Harry and Eddie shooting the breeze.

The atmosphere immediately changed when Eddie stopped saying "Harry" and switched to, "Mr. President…".

His friend's posture immediately stiffened.

"Mr. President," Eddie repeated, "In regard to Palestine, and the position of the US, I wish you would reconsider ----"

"Reconsider? Reconsider!" Truman exclaimed. "I won't reconsider nothing! You have no idea what I've been going through! It's those Jews! They come in here, not asking politely, but demanding! And that big rabbi from Cleveland even slammed his hand down right here on the president's desk. Can you imagine? Shouting at the president about what he wants done and when? While half of the American Jews have an opposite idea. The moment they leave my office they run to the reporters and turn it all around. You don't know how those 'blankety-blank-blank' East Coast Heebs are!"

In a loud voice he continued to spout the most inflammatory things about the Jews.

> **"Men make history and not the other way around. In periods where there is no leadership, society stands still. Progress occurs when courageous, skillful leaders seize the opportunity to change things for the better." Truman**

Eddie's notes read,

"This man, who I have always considered my finest lifelong friend, had suddenly become as close to being the worst anti-Semite I ever ran into. I couldn't believe I was actually hearing what he was saying."

Eddie's written account continued, *"I assumed and feared it was the end of our relationship. Tears began rolling down my cheeks. I knew there was no arguing with him or any chance of changing his Missouri-mule mind. But just then I saw it. It was on a table next to the wall. It was a replica of the statue that stands in front of the courthouse in Independence. It was*  *Andrew Jackson on horseback. This little statue was a replica of the big one Harry had installed when he was the Jackson County judge. I hoped that this replica of Andrew Jackson could be the turning point. I went over and put my hand on his sacred little statue. I looked at the president and said, "Harry, [no more "Mr. President"] when we had our store together, you were always in the backroom reading books about Andrew Jackson. You're probably the best-read man in the world on Andrew Jackson. You even built a statue to him when you were the county judge. I know how much Andrew Jackson has meant to you. He always was your hero and I'm going to tell you something, Harry, I've got a hero too. His name is Chaim Weizmann. I think he is the greatest Jew in the world. I know you met him last November one time, Harry, I know you did. And now you refuse to see him. He came all the way from Palestine with just the hope that you would see him again for just a few minutes. Harry, he's an old man, he's sick and going blind;*

Andrew Jackson (1767 – 1845) was an American soldier and seventh President of the United States from 1829 to 1837. As president, Jackson sought to advance the rights of the "common man" against a "corrupt aristocracy" and to preserve the Union.

he's in a hospital bed in a hotel in New York City. He came to see you for five or ten minutes. He's probably dying, Harry! He came all this way to tell you what the facts really are, and you are refusing his simple request for a few minutes of your time. Maybe what's behind all this is because you got your feelings hurt because some arrogant rabbi slammed his hand down on your desk. Harry, I know this is the toughest job in the world, but boy, I never knew you could be this thin skinned. My people have already had six million killed, all I'm asking for in this life and death situation in Palestine is that you would listen to Dr. Weizmann for a few minutes and he will give you the truth about what is happening over there."

His face reddening, Truman glared at Eddie, plunked himself down in his chair, drummed his fingers on the desk, spun around and stared out the window. Having no idea how long he would be ignored by the president, Eddie wondered if he should leave. Had he been dismissed? But then he realized that Harry was thinking and afterwards, he could not recall how long this impasse lasted.

Slowly, Harry turned around. Staring at Eddie through those thick glasses he then proceeded to speak the most endearing words Eddie ever heard a man say, "Alright, you old bald-headed S.O.B! You win! I'll see him!"

Five days later, on Thursday March 18, Chaim Weizmann was ushered into the White House through a little-known back entrance. The originally requested few-minutes meeting turned into a relatively long session. At this meeting, the future 1st president of Israel elegantly and eloquently touched the heart and soul of the 33rd US President.

As a result, Truman said, "Not only will the US vote for partition in the UN, but we'll be honored to be the first to recognize the State of Israel when it is declared. And CHIME*, you have my word and handshake on that!"

[Truman's Missouri midwestern twang made it impossible to say "Chaim", which always sounded like "Chime." Weizmann later wrote that he enjoyed the no-nonsense charm of the president.]

Here is a copy of the letter Truman signed when the State of Israel was declared on the 14th of May 1948 at 11 minutes after 6 p.m.

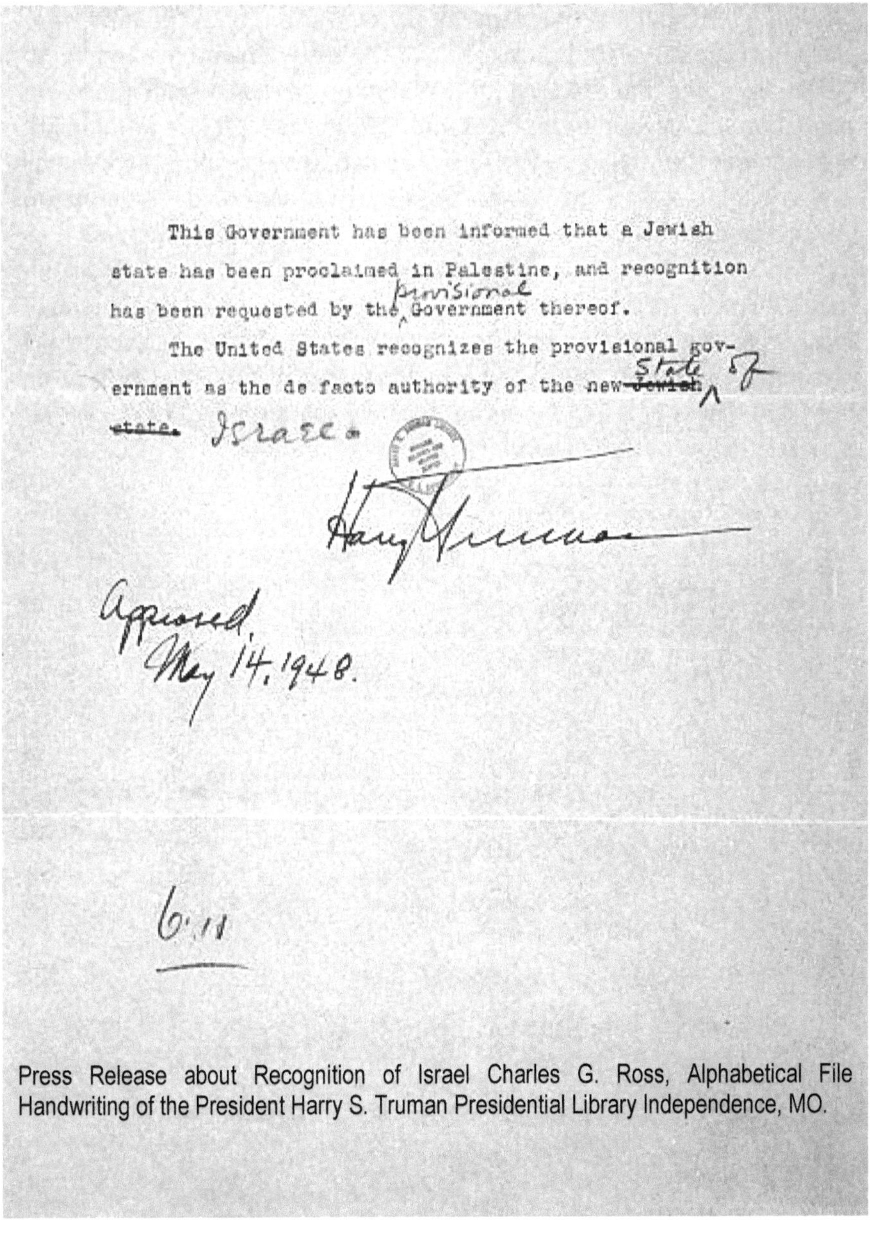

This Government has been informed that a Jewish state has been proclaimed in Palestine, and recognition has been requested by the provisional Government thereof.

The United States recognizes the provisional government as the de facto authority of the new ~~Jewish~~ State of ~~state.~~ Israel.

Harry Truman

Approved,
May 14, 1948.

6:11

Press Release about Recognition of Israel Charles G. Ross, Alphabetical File Handwriting of the President Harry S. Truman Presidential Library Independence, MO.

"The US recognizes the State of …" at the time the letter was typed no one at the White House knew what the new Jewish nation was going to be named. Just before the official signing word came that it's not the *"Jewish State"*, but it is the *"State of Israel."* Accordingly, the misnomer was scratched out by the president and the correct name penned in.

Eleven minutes after 6 PM in the time zone of Washington, DC corresponded to 11 minutes after midnight in Israel. It was at midnight in Israel that the legality of the Resignation of the Palestine Mandate by Great Britain took effect. This document of *de facto* recognition by the USA made America the first nation to recognize the State of Israel.

Harry Truman knew it was a key moment in time and a fulfillment of Prophecy. He knew what was written in Isaiah 66, "Who has ever heard of such things? Who has ever seen things like this? Can a country be born in a day or a nation be brought forth in a moment? Yet no sooner is Zion in labor than she gives birth to her children."

Clark Clifford, a young assistant to Truman who was present at the signing, wrote that Truman had several reasons for wanting to recognize the nascent state, not the least of which was,

" ... *he was a student and believer in the Bible since his youth. From his reading of the Old Testament he felt the Jews derived a legitimate historical right to Palestine, and he sometimes cited such Biblical lines as Deuteronomy 1:8: Behold, I have set the land before you: go in and possess the land which the Lord sware unto your fathers, Abraham, Isaac, and Jacob, to give unto them and to their seed after them.""*

The birth of the State of Israel was a watershed moment in history!
In a sense, **Chaim Weizmann, Harry Truman, Eddie Jacobson** (and many others whose names we will never know) were the mid-wives helping that baby into the modern world.

But above all, it was the 'hidden Hand of God' moving silently in the lives of all these people, bringing them together at the right time.
In believing they were doing the right thing those people became agents to bring God's Plan into fruition. Because of the immediate US recognition, the infant nation of the Jews gained world legitimacy.
For the first time, the Jewish State was able to legitimately purchase weapons to protect themselves and to be able to buy and sell with other countries.

When Harry Truman bucked the establishment and over-rode the objections of his own State Department and most of his Cabinet, everything changed. God blessed Harry Truman and our nation when he took that stand at that particular moment in time.

Once he stated, "I have the feeling that God has created us and brought us to our present position of power and strength for some great purpose."

Four years later, in 1952, Truman explained his attitude toward the State of Israel to Foreign Secretary Moshe Sharett. Sharett reported that Truman's view was "the result of his knowledge and study of Israel's history from the days of Abraham" and rested on the promises made to the Jewish people in the First World War (that is, the Balfour Declaration), which "must be kept."

Eddie probably never thought of himself as an "Esther," but like this heroic Jewish queen, neither did he remain silent when he could just as easily have mumbled an apology. He remembered an important lesson learned during the Great War - "Silence is Consent."

When Truman vented his frustration on him, he could have kept quiet and smoothed over the rift. But he didn't and because of that, Eddie is remembered and honored today.

Stand up and speak up for what you know is right and don't let the fear of future consequences shut you down!

Eddie found himself in a similar situation to the account in Esther 4:14,

"For if you remain silent at this time, Eddie, relief and deliverance for the Jews will arise from another place... And who knows but that you have come to your royal position for such a time as this?"

This story is an excellent example of a Jew (Abraham's descendant) and a Gentile, respecting each other, and working together all those years. God, in His great mosaic, used their friendship to unleash the blessings that had been promised to Abraham at least 3,000 years previously.

Remember that lawyer in Kansas City who was awakened in the middle of the night and asked if he knew Eddie Jacobson?

Mr. **A.J. Granoff** had the privilege of accompanying Eddie several times to the Oval Office for meetings with the president.

Granoff's letters to his son describe his impressions of what Truman did for Israel and especially for the United States.

He wrote, *"When the truth is finally told, I may say here about Harry Truman's contribution toward a Jewish State, his name above all others in the Christian world, will by the Jewish people everywhere be blessed in their temples and synagogues. About this I'm as sure as anyone could possibly be. What's more, his contribution was the vital factor which swung the U.N. General Assembly toward the 33 to 13 vote on November 29th — and in the face of heart breaking complications and problems.... There was not the slightest semblance toward currying the favor of Jews or anybody else. 'It was best for the United States' — and he lets it go at that — while others are claiming the credit."*

In an interview with Eddie's daughter, Elinor F. Borenstine, about her father's role in the recognition of the State of Israel, she recalled,

"Daddy's role became even more important (after recognition) because there was no ambassador yet. Every bit of business that was done between Israel and the United States went through Eddie Jacobson. It came through our living room. Years later, Daddy said to me, "You know, I spend all this money going to and from Washington with all of this business for the new little State. I won't have anything to leave you." And I said, "Daddy, you're leaving me the best thing of all. This is quite a heritage I have."

Indeed, it is!

The schoolboy always remained in the man that Harry Truman grew to be. When he became president of the United States on April 12, 1945, he was—to some degree, in some important ways—the same person he had been when growing up in Independence.

As the years went by, he changed in appearance, but the qualities of character remained.

Truman and his mother

Those beliefs shaped the policies of Truman's administration, our nation and eventually that of the world.

Harry continued to be the 'good boy' in his teacher's classroom. Inside the president was a young man who understood that in real life, people were not always what they were supposed to be, and that well-reasoned common sense was the key to decision making, stopping that buck and dealing with it.

Thank God for putting a plain-spoken common man in the White House at the appointed time. His actions brought a blessing to the Jewish people and to the nation of Israel AND to our own nation by doing the right thing at the right time.

Good for a Laugh

President Truman congratulates President Weizmann.
"I am president of 140 million people, you are now
president over one million people."
"You are wrong, sir," Weizman replies. "I have become
president over a million presidents!"

TRUMAN QUOTES

- It is amazing what you can accomplish if you do not care who gets the credit.
- I never gave anybody hell! I just told the truth and they thought it was hell.
- In reading the lives of great men, I found that the first victory they won was over themselves... self-discipline with all of them came first.
- You can never get all the facts from just one newspaper, and unless you have all the facts, you cannot make proper judgements about what is going on.

More Truman Quotes:

- You can always amend a big plan, but you can never expand a little one. I don't believe in little plans. I believe in plans big enough to meet a situation which we can't possibly foresee now.
- All the president is, is a glorified public relations man who spends his time flattering, kissing, and kicking people to get them to do what they are supposed to do
- I had faith in Israel before it was established, I have faith in it now. I believe it has a glorious future before it - not just another sovereign nation, but as an embodiment of the great ideals of our civilization.

PART 2

Lyndon Baines Johnson

Lyndon Baines Johnson (1908 – 1973)

Lyndon, often referred to by the initials LBJ, was an American politician from Texas who served as the 36th president of the United States from 1963 to 1969. Johnson is one of only four people who have served in all four federal elected positions: United States Representative, United States Senator, Vice president and President.

Introduction

This part contains a series of snapshots of the larger-than-life career of Lyndon B. Johnson, the 36th president of the United States and the fourth to be elevated to office by assassination. By focusing on seemingly trivial events we can see a shadowy pattern of an unseen hand maneuvering him into the Oval Office – a place he passionately desired to be one day. Johnson's own futile efforts never would have propelled him there. It is only at the conclusion of his outsized life that these disparate puzzle pieces are seen as a part of God's bigger plan.

It should go without saying that no president of the United States has been, is, or will be perfect. Many people (myself included) proudly state that their political views and votes are determined by the character and personal ethics of the candidates. However, as the 2016 presidential race started winnowing out the candidates, had I held onto my preconceived criteria, I would have had no one to vote for. After all the speeches I had made encouraging Christian church-goers to get up out of their pews and vote, this was an embarrassing situation.

I had blamed them for not being politically involved enough to get someone with their values into office. Then, Mike Huckabee, the former Governor of Arkansas, put it all in perspective for me. Speaking to people who were hesitant to vote for presidential candidate Trump he said, "Hey, we're not electing a Sunday School teacher here!" That resonated with me.

"Let me quote a famous politician, Barack Obama, who said, 'Elections have consequences.' They certainly do!"
–Mike Huckabee

I began to think about the type of person that God called to extricate Israel from the oppression and existential dangers they had gotten themselves into. There was outcast warrior Jephthah, leading Israel to victory both internally and externally. (Judges 10-12). Gideon also came to mind as a man of courage who took a stand against the religious mores of his family and community. He violated one of the principles of warfare (overwhelming force) by sending most of his army away from the battlefield. He held grudges and was certainly a violent man. (Judges 6-8). Moses, of course, is another example of an escaped murderer who was called at an advanced age to lead the nation out of slavery.

By our present-day unrealistic standards, few of those leaders who rescued Israel would be elected today. History shows that desperate nations often wait too long for the perfect leader who can pass muster as a Sunday School Superintendent. Actually, the last Sunday School teacher who became president turned out to be one of the worst ones when it came to his Israel support record. (Did you hear that, Jimmy?)

In Biblical accounts and our own political history, it seems that God often selects the most unqualified of individuals to lead the country. Perhaps He does this because He wants us to acknowledge that He is still alive, engaged and very much on His Throne; that He can remove or elevate anyone He wants to - including democratically elected presidents. (Daniel 2:21, Psalm 75:7, Proverbs 8:15-16)
Our task is to pray for our leaders and for wisdom for ourselves.
(1 Tim 2: 1-3, James 1:5) Maybe democratic elections are already fixed in Heaven and we are just given an opportunity to show by voting where we stand spiritually.

The next president we investigate had many similar childhood experiences to those of Harry Truman. Both were born in tiny houses in the country and were the firstborn sons in their families. Their farmer fathers had an interest in politics with big, elusive dreams, but neither were good businessmen.

When a reporter said something about his father being a failure, Harry Truman sharply cut the man down to size by telling him, *"My father was not a failure! After all, he was the father of a President of the United States."* LBJ could have said the same thing.

Seeds are no Small Thing

In every person's life, little seeds are planted. Someone may say something to you which you don't get at first. Maybe you don't even think about it for many years. But it was planted and though it may seem dormant, it isn't dead. The little seed planted in little Lyndon's mind eventually grew into something big and powerful.

To begin the story, we have to go back to the Civil War. Samuel ("Big" Sam) Ealy, one of the tall Johnson boys, moved from Alabama to the hill country of Texas. When the war started Sam saddled his horse and rode off to join the Confederate Cavalry. Sam saw a few battles along the Texas border and later in life, his veteran status gave him credibility during his foray into Texas politics.

When "Big Sam" returned following the Confederate surrender, he rejoined his brothers in a venture to buy cattle and drive them up the Chisolm Trail to market in Kansas.

The **Chisholm Trail** was a trail used in the post-Civil War era to drive cattle overland, from ranches in Texas to Kansas railheads. The portion of the trail marked by Jesse Chisholm went from his southern trading post near the Red River, to his northern trading post near Kansas City, Kansas.

Although the bottom dropped out of the Texas cattle business after a couple of years, Big Sam managed to hold onto some farmland in the hill country west of Austin. One of the nearby settlements was Stonewall, Texas, named in honor of the famous Confederate General.

In this picture, Big Sam stands out in front of the "dog trot" house that he built. Next to big Sam is his wife Eliza and the girl with the defiant look is their daughter Jessie. Years later, Jessie Johnson married a man named Hatcher, so we will refer to her as Aunt Jessie Hatcher.

Aunt Jessie is really the unsung heroine of this story because she was the outspoken Jew-loving, Bible-believing aunt who hovered over her nephew and kept the future president in line (all of his life) when it came to the issue of the Jews and Israel.

As a young lady Jessie became sister-in-law to the future president's mother, Rebekah Baines, who had married Jessie's older brother, Sam Jr. Jessie was still single when Lyndon was born on the next-door ranch with the Pedernales River practically running through the front yard.

Later, Jessie recalled the years that she helped Rebekah in raising little Lyndon. "When you feed a little kid, bathe him, change his diapers, and put him to bed, all that sort of things - it's hard to think of him as anything more than a barefoot Hill Country boy - no matter what else he grows up to be."

This is a true story of Lyndon Baines Johnson who was raised amongst a Christadelphian family. During his childhood, the seed of love for the Jews was planted. It developed to the degree that he helped change the course of Israel's history in one of their darkest hours.

In 2010, **Stonewall, Texas** population was 525. It was named after Confederate General Stonewall Jackson, by Israel P. Nunez, who established a stage station near the site in 1870. Thomas Jonathan Stonewall Jackson (1824 –1863) was a Southern general during the American Civil War, and the best-known Confederate commander after General Robert E. Lee. He played an important part in winning many significant battles. President Lyndon B. Johnson was born and died on the same ranch located nearby Stonewall.

President Johnson's birthplace in Gillespie County. Rt. Outhouse at Johnson birthplace

"When I was young, poverty was so common that we didn't know it had a name." LBJ

The **Christadelphians** are a millenarian Christian group who hold a view of Biblical Unitarianism. Originating in the United Kingdom and North America in the 19th century around the teachings of John Thomas, the name Christadelphian was taken from the Greek for "Brethren in Christ".

In the fall of 1879, a traveling minister of the Christadelphian faith visited Central Texas. Preacher Oatman stopped at the Sam Johnson farm for the night and discussed the Bible during and after dinner.

Theological debates were common in that era and Sam arranged an all-day debate between the Christadelphian preacher and his own Disciples of Christ minister. The little church was packed, as everybody wanted to hear these two men. One of the questions that came up was: "Will the Jews ever go back to Israel?"

The Disciples of Christ preacher said, "No way. They rejected Jesus. They are doomed to wander – they are the wandering Jews. They are never going back because all of those promises that God made to the Jews now belong to us. We are the Church. They rejected Jesus, so God is through with them. There is no plan for them anymore."

The Christadelphian responded, "Absolutely! The Jews are going back! They must go back because God's Word says they are going to be back! There are at least 141 promises stating, 'I'm going to bring back those Jews to MY land.' God calls it MY LAND eight times in the Bible. And when I call my Chosen People back into that land things are really going to pop and happen."

Big Sam stood up and may have exclaimed, "This here Christadelphian fellow is right! God's Word says so. I tell you what, preacher, I'm quitting this here church!"

Which he did! In 1879, 41-year-old "Big" Sam was baptized and became a lifelong Christadelphian.

Little Jessie and eventually her brother Sam Jr., the father of Lyndon, and many of the rest of Sam's family also joined the Christadelphians. Throughout their lives, they always stood for the Biblical fact that God was going to bring those Jews back into the Promised Land.

It makes sense that little Lyndon, sitting on his grandfather's knee, listened to him say, "Lyndon! Take care of the Jews, God's chosen people. Consider them your friends and help them any way you can."

The fact is that Big Sam's farm was so far out in the country that there was probably not a Jew within 60 miles from where they lived. For the first five years of his life, young Lyndon and his parents lived just half a mile down the road from his grandparent's house. Some of Lyndon's fondest memories involved walking along the banks of the Pedernales to that house. His grandfather would give him a stick of peppermint candy or an apple, tell him stories about the Civil War or the cattle drives. And finally, he climbed up on his big gray horse and returned the boy to his worried mother.

During his presidency, Lyndon often mentioned his grandfather's admonition, "Lyndon! You take care of the Jews ... and you help them in any way you can."

In 1915, seventy-five-year-old Sam Ealy Johnson Sr. contracted pneumonia. On his deathbed he "spoke to his loved ones, assuring them of his complete readiness to meet his Maker and of his sustaining hope of eternal life."

His grave lies only steps from that of his grandson in the Johnson family plot at the LBJ Ranch.

Even though his seven year old grandson didn't know any Jews, one day, the seed his grandfather implanted would sprout.

Johnson family at the Ranch, with Aunt Jessie. Today, the rebuilt house stands on the same spot where LBJ was born.

As time went by, something else happened to Lyndon. It had to do with Psalm 37: "Delight thyself also in the Lord: and He shall give thee the desires of your heart."

Many people who read this verse may think, "Well.... God won't give me the desires of my heart. I know that those desires aren't proper; as a matter of fact, they are probably evil. So, there must be something wrong here." But, while meditating on the words and delighting themselves in the Lord, they begin to realize that it is God who puts those godly desires into the heart. And understand that God doesn't tease us either. If He put a desire into your heart, then He will also make a way for it to come to pass. But, it takes at least one step of faith toward the fulfillment of that desire. And when that happens, all you have to do is enjoy the ride, because God always brings that desire to pass - in His own incredible way.

The other part of Psalms 37 says, "Commit thy way unto the Lord; trust also in Him; and He shall bring it to pass."

Bring what to pass? Those very desires that He put into your heart in the first place.

From an early age, while sitting there on that porch, Lyndon had the desire in his heart to become President of the United States. There is a story that on the day Lyndon was born, his grandfather rode his horse through Johnson City, shouting, "The future Texas Senator has just been born on the banks of the Pedernales!"

Maybe just being a senator was the starting point in the electoral desire that his grandfather was heralding. It is reported that even in grade school Lyndon was already announcing his future plans to move into the White house. Lyndon's heart's desire drove him, all of his life.

In many ways, the Sam Jr. and Rebekah Johnson family resembled the John and Martha Truman family. Both families had college educated mothers who were adamant about their future president's education. Oddly enough, one of those sons never attended college and the other graduated from a small and relatively unknown school. Both their fathers were farmers who had a tough time making a go of their land. Lyndon's family was poor. When his father hit hard times on the ranch the family had to move into town – Johnson City.

> **Johnson City,** founded by James Polk Johnson, nephew of Samuel Ealy Johnson, Sr. and uncle to President Johnson. James P. Johnson donated a 320-acre site on the Pedernales River for the founding of the town in 1879.

The family could not even afford the rent on the house, which was located at the far edge of town. Family members provided Sam Jr. with the rent money; and Aunt Jessie Hatcher was always around to help in many ways.

People thought the Johnson family was arrogant and that didn't sit well in small town Texas, especially because Lyndon was always telling everyone: "One day I'm going to be President of the U.S."
Townspeople thought they acted overly pompous. "Even when they are sitting, the Johnson's strut," they said. "They think too much of themselves," others criticized.
The big, loud and brash Lyndon didn't keep his thoughts to himself. The whole family was outspoken on certain issues that weren't very popular in Johnson City, Texas.
As a young boy, Lyndon watched his politically active grandfather "Big Sam" and father "Little Sam" seek clemency for Leo Frank, an innocent Jewish scapegoat falsely accused in a child's murder in Georgia.
In 1915, Leo Frank was lynched by a mob and the local Texas Ku Klux Klan threatened to kill the outspoken Johnsons. Lyndon's family hid in an earthen cellar while his father and uncles, anticipating a KKK attack on their home, stood guard with shotguns on their porch.
Johnson's speech writer, Horace Busby, stated, "Johnson often cited Leo Frank's lynching as the source of his opposition to anti-Semitism."
Undoubtedly, everything Lyndon also heard from his Christadelphian family members about always blessing the Jews was highlighted when Jewish Leo Frank was lynched in Georgia.

While researching the facts in Lyndon's life, this writer realized that there were many versions of the most inconsequential incidents. After reading the same incident from several sources, I realized that it was LBJ himself who was retelling the same story in different ways. He never let the facts get in the way of telling a good story which put him in a better light. No matter how big and intimidating and powerful he was in the eyes of others, it was never enough to fill the emptiness in his soul. As Texas author Clinton Rossiter wrote, "LBJ was a breeding ground of an indestructible myth."

Numerous times (never publicly known) during his rise to power and even during his presidency, he would be so incapacitated by his fears that he would crawl into bed and pull the covers over his head.

Lady Bird always had to come to the rescue and talk him out of these funks. Without her help it is possible that he never would have been re-elected to any office.

He was an incredibly complicated man. But once again, we conclude that God can and will use anyone He cares to. Perhaps it is done to remind us that His ways are not our ways, and that anyone can be used of God. And that it really doesn't matter how many brownie points you may think you've earned. Moses, Gideon, David, Joseph and millions of other un-named individuals were just going about their business when God gave them a new assignment.

The reason we are studying these presidents is because they answered when they were called. And as they had the free will to choose, they made the right choice when it came to helping and blessing Israel.

When he needed the $75 tuition fee for Southwest Texas State Teachers College, San Marcos (it wasn't Harvard or Yale, not even the University of Texas just a local Teachers College) Lyndon borrowed the money from his Aunt Jessie. It is also possible that he took out a loan from the local bank and maybe there was even another story.

The problem with Lyndon was that he was totally inconsistent with the true details of his life. The deeper one digs into the early life of Lyndon, the more contradictions, half-truths and full-blown lies surface.

After trying to document some rather inconsequential event, like how he came up with $75 college fees, one is overwhelmed by the myriad of stories he constructed. All these prevarications were designed to make himself look bigger, better, tougher, smarter, etc. than he really was. He became so skillful at weaving these stories together that it is probable that he no longer knew the truth from his own fiction. Often, after trying to run one of these minor stories to ground, a writer may conclude, "What does it matter anyway how he got the $75?"

It is unknown as to whether Lyndon ever studied or even read Machiavelli's *The Prince,* but his famous argument about the lack of value in telling the truth was either inherited in his DNA or he was just a natural.

Machiavelli argued, *"Everyone admits how praiseworthy it is in a prince to keep his word, and to behave with integrity rather than cunning. Nevertheless, our experience has been that those princes who have done great things have considered keeping their word of little account and have to know how to beguile men's minds by shrewdness and cunning. In the end these princes have overcome those who have relied on keeping their word."*

So, no matter how he got the $75 tuition, he could have easily obtained it from his father. However, Lyndon seemed to be perpetually at war with him and I don't think he would have lowered himself to ask him for a loan. Lyndon did enter San Marcos and his story was that he took every campus job he could possibly get. He said he worked as a janitor, a gardener and finally as secretary to the college president.

However, the college president does recall receiving numerous phone calls from Lyndon's mother always pestering him for a better job for her boy. His time in school wasn't exactly the Horatio Alger tale of an impoverished boy making good. He craved the power involved in politics, even if it was only student government.

However, by the time he was a junior he didn't have enough money nor could he borrow any to go back to school. Instead, he accepted a job as a school teacher in the town of Cotulla, a predominantly Mexican town in south Texas.

Lyndon Baines Johnson (seated center) and his first students at the Welhausen School in Cotulla, Texas, 1928.

Teaching there for a year, he realized that, as poor as he may have thought he was, it was nothing compared to the dead end faced by the kids that he taught. Because he had this first-hand experience working with those Mexican children, his liberal beliefs about education, dignity, democracy and helping people rise up were genuine.

Years later, when Lyndon was criticized for "doing the liberal thing," most folks didn't realize it was part and parcel of who he really was.

After graduating from San Marcos, Lyndon taught for a few weeks in Pearsall, Texas, and then took a job teaching public speaking at Sam Houston High School in Houston. He boarded with Aunt Jessie who conveniently lived there and always reminded him of her Christadelphian beliefs. She also joined the Zionist Organization of America.

While in Houston, Lyndon became involved in local politics, which he greatly enjoyed. He was fascinated with the challenge and he perfected techniques in trying to awaken and convince people about the issues. After getting his feet wet in the Houston area he heard about a congressional contest in south Texas. Because of the death-in-office of the Republican incumbent, Richard Kleberg (an acquaintance of Lyndon's father and an heir of the King Ranch) was running for Congress as a Democrat.

> **King Ranch**, located in South Texas between Corpus Christi and Brownsville near Kingsville, is the largest ranch in Texas, comprising 825,000 acres (3,340 km2; 1,289 sq mi). it was founded in 1853 by Captain Richard King and Gideon K. Lewis. The ranch does not consist of one single contiguous plot of land, but rather four large sections called divisions. Since 1961 the area has become a National Historic Landmark.

At that time, the King Ranch certainly was the richest and largest ranch in the USA with nearly a million acres, scores of cattle herds and oil wells both in the US and even abroad.

Richard Mifflin Kleberg Sr. (1887 –1955), a Democrat, was a seven-term member of the United States House of Representatives from Texas's 14th congressional district over the period 1931–1945 and an heir to the King Ranch in South Texas. He was first elected in 1931 in a special election after the death of Harry M. Wurzbach and was elected unopposed in 1940 and 1942.

US Representative Kleberg evidently didn't like the work of real politics that much, so he didn't feel the need to spend an inordinate amount of time at the office. Kleberg sensed that Lyndon was lean and hungry for the day-to-day drudgery of political life and he hired him to be his legislative secretary.

The tall, gangly, loud and brash assistant moved to Washington DC, only to realize that the congressman hardly ever showed up at the office. Lyndon became the *defacto* congressman and carried himself like he was the congressman. It is reported that, when speaking on the phone he often passed himself off as Richard Kleberg.

His drive, ambition, and competence made him stand out among the other young staffers in Washington at that time. Their unofficial group was named the 'Little Congress.' Lyndon quickly got to know all the other congressional staff members that were about his age and he 'campaigned hard' for election as president of that 'Little Congress' by utilizing the same techniques he would hone to perfection when he ran for 'real' offices.

Working for a congressman more interested in golf and polo than in legislating gave the young aide the opportunity to take charge and make himself known. In short order, Lyndon was directing the work of Kleberg's staff. He reverted to his childhood modus operandi of bossing and driving and demanding endless hours of work from others just as he did with his younger sisters and brothers in Johnson City. In those first months in DC he not only learned how Washington politics worked, but he also got himself elected Speaker of the Little Congress, an association of House staff secretaries.

Lyndon revealed his ability to read a situation and take advantage of a loophole others had missed. In this way he took over the Little Congress before anyone figured out what he was up to. Until Lyndon arrived on the scene, the election of officers was dictated and based on seniority. By inviting a large contingent of congressional employees, such as elevator operators and mailmen to join the Little Congress, he fooled everyone who started the organization.

Johnson's tactic expanded the membership beyond congressional secretaries. According to the organization's bylaws, eligibility included anyone on the legislative payroll which paved the way for his surprise election as Speaker. This was the best of Texas county politics in action and he was fast becoming a master of the art.

It was there that LBJ began to utilize the persuasive tactics that were later coined the 'Johnson treatment.' The six foot four Johnson would lean close to a staffer (or later a Senator), towering over his 'prey' and bending them backwards, whether speaking softly and cajoling, flattering or threatening to expose their hidden foibles, or even bribing, until he won the promise of their vote.

He was always searching for untapped sources of influence and power in Kleberg's district as well as anywhere in the state of Texas that could help him advance to the next stage in his drive for the top.

He assiduously courted those in local positions of power, which was to characterize Johnson's political life from then on. Lyndon cultivated a friendship with Texas Congressman Sam Rayburn by ingratiating himself with Mr. Sam as the 'son' the Speaker never had. Anyone who could be of some future service to Lyndon knew him by then, because by entering a room like a tornado, everyone present knew Lyndon had arrived. His father and grandfather had used the same techniques in Austin and Lyndon was perfecting it into a political art form.

Whether they liked him or not, no one ever forgot an encounter with the 'Texas Tornado.' He was quoted as saying, "If you're in politics and you can't tell when you walk into a room who's for you and who's against you, then you're in the wrong line of work."

Lyndon was in Austin, Texas mending political fences for his boss when he met a lovely young lady, 21-year-old Claudia Taylor. During their first date Johnson talked the entire time. "Can I have another breakfast date tomorrow?" he asked her. He spent the next whole day with her and kept on talking, talking, talking. Despite being swept off her feet, Claudia held back when Lyndon wanted to marry her right away. During their courtship he brought her a book of essays, written just after Hitler had risen to power in Germany in 1933. The book, *Nazism: An assault on Civilization,* was accurately predicting what Hitler's future plans were, even though the war and the killing of Jews were years in the future. This showed Claudia where his mind was. He often had the uncanny ability to think ahead to future events. For someone courting it was an unusual gift, but that was Lyndon - unconventional, to say the least!

When he met Claudia, Lyndon was still the secretary to the Congressman. They were really a pair made for each other and without her, Lyndon would never have become the man that he would be.

What Claudia had to put up with in the future was almost unbelievable, but they were a perfect match. He couldn't have had a stronger woman behind him than the tough as nails 'Lady Bird'.

He was especially intrigued by her nickname – 'Lady Bird' because her initials would also be LBJ. By this time, he was using his three initials as a brand, just like FDR (and later JFK).

90 letters in 90 days

In years to come all his daughters also were branded with the LBJ initials (Lynda Bird and Lucy Baines as well as his dog, "Little Beagle" Johnson).

Honeymoon

There is little doubt that he was served well by the perfect wife who had been prepared early in life for him by having a domineering father who had many of the same peculiarities as the man she married.

Their marriage and the marriage of their parents on both sides would have hardly been described as ones 'made in heaven' but it seemed to have been one that Texas horse breeders would have understood. The weaknesses in the line of the sire were matched by the strengths on the side of the dam. Johnson's bluster, boorishness, and insensitivity were healed by her steel magnolia-like southern sweetness, hospitality and soothing sensitivity to those he hurt.

Presidential historians will continue to puzzle over how one man of humble origins could combine such prodigious quantities of good and evil, insight and self-delusion. LBJ was plagued by self-doubts and fears all of his life, and his bragging and bullying were a cover-up to keep those who were intimidated by his actions from getting too close and having a glimpse into his tormented soul.

"It was a pronounced, prolonged depression," opined Bill Moyers, LBJ's Press Secretary. "He would just go within himself, just disappear - morose, self-pitying, angry ... He was a tormented man."

Lyndon described himself to Moyers as being in a Louisiana swamp that was "pulling me down."

"When he said it," Moyers remembers, "he was lying in bed with the covers almost above his head."

Of course, none of this bizarre behavior was ever revealed to the public or even known by most of his staff.

After his marriage, Johnson became even more impatient in seeking wider career horizons. He was appointed Texas State Director of the National Youth Administration, an FDR New Deal agency designed to help students to stay in school. After four years of service Lyndon left the laidback Congressman Kleberg's office, who hated to see his most energetic staffer depart in a cloud of dust. Ten years later, when Kleberg needed Lyndon's help in a tight election, his former aide was nowhere to be found and Kleberg was defeated. In the depths of the Depression, Johnson wangled the NYA appointment and escaped the staffer job through connections he had been cultivating in DC. An important connection was the old Texan bachelor Sam Rayburn, who later became the Speaker of the House for a record 17 years while LBJ ascended to the Senate Majority Leader.

Between 1935 and 1939 the **National Youth Administration (NYA),** sponsored by Roosevelt, focused on providing work and education for Americans between the ages of 16 and 25. The NYA was dissolved in 1943. College youth were paid from $6 to $40 a month for "work study" projects at their schools. Children from relief families were paid $10 to $25 a month for part-time work that included job training. The NYA operated several programs for out of school youth.

This Texas NYA position, a federal youth-employment program, connected him into the grassroots of Texas politics. It included all the counties of the state and allowed him entree into the local Democratic power structures in every corner of Texas. When the US Congressman from the Texas 10th District, Buck Buchanan, suddenly died from a heart attack, Lyndon immediately announced for that office before the corpse had even cooled.

The successful years in that NYA job gave him the tailwind he needed for the special election in 1937. LBJ campaigned under the clever

banner that proclaimed "Franklin D. and Lyndon B." implying a closeness that didn't yet exist. The special election was held on the 10th of April, 1937. Lyndon bested nine other candidates by winning 28% (a plurality) of the votes cast. Not only had he outworked his opponents by a long shot, but he also outraised and outspent them. It was estimated that more than $100,000 was spent on the election. At that time, it was by far the most expensive Depression era congressional race in Texas history.

"Until justice is blind to color, until education is unaware of race, until opportunity is unconcerned with the color of men's skins, emancipation will be a proclamation but not a fact." LBJ

"I believe the destiny of your generation - and your nation - is a rendezvous with excellence." LBJ

Shimeon Novodvorsky Becomes Jim Novy

One of the first persons Lyndon turned to for support was a Jewish gentleman in Austin by the name of Jim Novy.

On Yom Kippur in 1913 – 24 years earlier - a penniless 17 year old Orthodox Jew named Shimeon Novodvorsky disembarked after a long sea voyage at Galveston, Texas. Coincidentally, it was the same year of the trial and lynching of the Jewish industrialist Leo Frank. Across the South, anti-Semitism and immigrant hatred was on the rise, and those who spoke against it, were threatened by the KKK.

Between 1907 and 1914, **Galveston** was the port city on the Gulf of Mexico which became home to a U.S. immigration assistance program operated by several Jewish organizations. The program was designed to divert Jewish immigrants fleeing Russia and eastern Europe, away from East Coast cities, particularly New York, which was already overcrowded with too many poverty-stricken immigrants. During its operation, ten thousand Jewish immigrants passed through the port.

Federal Immigration Station, Pelican Island, Galveston, about 1913.

A local rabbi met Shimeon at the dock and helped him get to Ennis, Texas where he joined his two older brothers.

He was the third brother (of eleven children) that his Polish father had sent to *Die Goldene Medina*, the Yiddish term for the USA, where the 'streets were paved with gold'.

The economic situation in Poland was getting worse as entangling treaties were inadvertently leading to the Great World War. At the same time, pogroms against the Jews were increasing. Shimeon was to join his brothers' newly started junk business.

"Listen, Shimeon," his brothers said, "nobody in Texas will be able to pronounce your name, Shimeon Novodvorsky." After a little thought they modified his old country name to a more Texas sounding handle like Jim Novy.

"OK, I'll be Jim if I have to be. Let's get to work." Shimeon responded.

The brothers bought scrap metal, built something from it or polished it up and resold it. They made a penny here and a nickel there. Over the years, these brothers became owners of a theater and then a chain of theaters all over Texas. In a few years of dogged work, they were making a lot of money. Their scrap metal business prospered during World War I. The start of a small fortune for the immigrant brothers eventually brought them into Texas political activity.

In 1937, Jim became a patron and contributor to Johnson during his first foray into elected public office. Their friendship blossomed and for the rest of their lives they worked together on different projects and were always ready to help each other.

This is the story of a Christian and a Jew respecting, cooperating and being a blessing to one another - the very essence of this book.

He Gets Things Done - -

Lyndon Johnson

Knows Washington

WHEN
JOHNSON RESIGNED
FROM NYA

Aubrey Williams, NYA administrator and Johnson had been a "first class job" and turned him "out of the oldest Mule Ditch here we have had."
- Associated Press from Washington

for **CONGRESSMAN**
10TH DISTRICT

Support the Man Who—
Stands with the President and for the People
Stands Whole-heartedly on Democratic platform of 1936
Understands Departmental Routine of Washington
Will Carry Colorado and Brazos Projects Through
Capably Administered His Part of the Roosevelt Program for Texas

Jim Novy (1896 –1971) was an Austin, Texas businessman, entrepreneur, and philanthropist. The wealthy scrap metal businessman became a philanthropist, partial to Jewish causes and a patron to numerous political figures; most notably he supported the career of Lyndon B. Johnson. He became an important figure in Austin politics and with his connection to Johnson he had influence all the way to the White House and Israel.

By the time Lyndon was ready to run for Congress, Jim was an important wealthy member of the Austin community. He was one of the first people to say to Lyndon, "Yes, I'm going to help you and back you as you run for Congress."

On May 11, just one month after his stunning victory in the special election, the newly minted Congressman Lyndon Johnson drove down to Galveston.

President Roosevelt had decided it was time to go fishing in the Gulf of Mexico. When politicians go on a vacation, they make it look like they're doing governmental business. Democrat FDR called ahead to the Democratic Governor of Texas, Allred, "I want to get off my boat at Galveston, then hop on a train. Make it happen."

Of course, Allred responded, "Yes sir, yes sir, (three bags full), we can do it."

The next thing Governor Allred did was to call the mayor of Galveston. "FDR is coming. This is going to be a great thing for the city of Galveston and the state of Texas. I want you to get things all spruced up. I want you to paint the bridge, I want you to make it look great because we are going to welcome the president there. This is very important for the Democratic party."

The Mayor of Galveston replied, "Governor, you probably forgot, but I'm a Republican and don't really care that much for FDR and I don't care if my bridge is kind of rusty when he comes."

After Alfred had slammed down the receiver, he called back a few minutes later. "Listen, Mayor, I've just been thinking about it. Here's what we are going to do. Not only are we going to paint that bridge, the state will do it, we're going to repave that road and we are going to fix everything up. There is one problem: we'll have to shut down that bridge for about six months, which will probably cripple your city."

The mayor of Galveston, who happened to be Jewish, got the message, "O.K. Governor, I get it. We're going to welcome FDR like he was a Republican when he arrives."

As soon as the word got out that FDR was going to stop in Texas, Lyndon frantically started calling around to find out when and where.

Being the opportunist that he was, Lyndon immediately drove down to Galveston, to welcome the president, get some 'face time' with the press and do his best to get into FDR's good graces.

At that time, not many people knew that FDR was crippled and could not stand unsupported. In this photo LBJ is to the far right.

In the next picture (below) the governor of Texas is no longer next to the President. He was undoubtedly elbowed out of the way by the brash rookie Congressman, who is now seen snuggling up to FDR.

The Governor kind of peeks in over the shoulder of Lyndon while he is schmoozing with FDR.

The mayor of Galveston, obviously not happy to be there, has been edited out of many of the pictures taken of this momentous event.

FDR, LBJ, Texas Governor James Allred, Galveston Mayor Adrian Levy. May 11, 1937

Remember the burning desire that was in the little country boy's heart to someday be the President?

Lyndon saw his time in Congress as just one of those steps on a long path. In 1941 he was rebuffed when he ran for the Senate but was able to keep his seat in the House. Everything he did was to get him to the big house at 1600 Pennsylvania Avenue.

The Tragic Voyage of the MS *St. Louis*

MS (*Motorschiff*) *St. Louis*, a diesel-powered passenger ship often incorrectly referred to as SS *St. Louis*; built in 1925 by Bremer Vulkan for the Hamburg America Line; St. Louis was built for both transatlantic liner service and for leisure cruises. It was most notable as the ship that carried Jewish refugees from Nazi Germany in 1939 in an unsuccessful emigration attempt; scrapped in Hamburg in 1952.

Return with us now to those pre-war ominous days of yesteryear, the Spring of 1939.

Blasting its foghorns and heading out into the Atlantic was a German-owned transatlantic passenger liner, the MS *St. Louis* bound for Havana, Cuba. She departed from the port of Hamburg with a human cargo of more than 900 persons, nearly all of

whom were hopeful Jews. That lovely Spring day, the 13th of May, seemed pregnant with hope for a bright future for those Jews who breathed a sigh of relief as they watched Hamburg slowly diminish over the ship's stern.

75

If only those passengers could have seen the dark war clouds forming just beyond the horizon on the eve of the forthcoming war, they may not have been so back-slapping congratulatory with each other as they stood on deck anticipating the start of a new life in a new land.

Hitler, already in power for six years, at that very moment was secretly planning his Nazi offensive against Poland in less than four months. That forthcoming *blitzkrieg* on 1 September would rapidly usher in the Second World War, which the League of Nations had 'guaranteed' would never happen. Until then, the war of 1914-1918 was known as the "Great War."
"WAR" had been outlawed and guarantees were in place to absolutely prevent another world-wide conflict. It was unthinkable to the Progressives that there could possibly be a "second" world war.
However, the war on the Jews had started in earnest as soon as Hitler entered office in 1933. Many Jews recognized that the doors of escape were quickly closing, and it was imperative that they and their loved ones escape Hitler's grasp.

The hopeful escapees outbound on the *St. Louis* had paid highly inflated prices for the landing certificates and transit visas. The Cuban representative in Germany greedily pocketed his hefty commission on each ticket, knowing full well that these documents most likely wouldn't be honored in Cuba without additional fees being demanded. The passengers knew nothing of the problems that awaited them in Cuba and that Cuban officials vied with each other in a continual scramble for bribes. Like other Central American countries, Cuba was also rife with general corruption in public service , and internal political power struggles. Under the surface the general malaise of a depressed economy was bubbling.
The passengers were also unaware of a recent hate-filled anti-Semitic rally attended by 40,000 Cubans, the largest in that country's history. It was held in Havana just a week before the *St. Louis* departed.
In order to leave a country that didn't even want them, the German Jewish citizens had to silently suffer innumerable indignities foisted on them by the Nazi bureaucrats who made them beg for the return of their personal documents.

Eventually, they would toss the German passports at them so they wouldn't have to touch the hands of 'dirty Jews'. Most of the passengers had previously been fired from their jobs and had to sell their personal property at bargain basement prices to their Teutonic neighbors. All of it - the humiliation and financial loss - had been cynically contrived by the Nazis in order to squeeze these unwanted Jews to pay their last farthing on their way out of the vaunted fatherland. With a stroke of a Jew-hating bureaucrat's pen, not only did they lose their status as German citizens, but they were abruptly changed to "stinking, unwanted stateless Jewish refugees."

After 14 days at sea the MS *St. Louis* finally entered Havana's port and dropped anchor. On deck, there were grateful cheers and hugs.
Everyone was relieved. They had lost their Germanic hearth and home, had been afraid and suffered heartache, but it had been worth it. The moment their ship received permission to dock they would enter a new world, safe from the Nazis and start that new life they had been dreaming of.

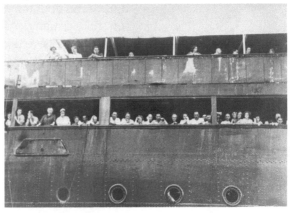

The Cuban government admitted 28 passengers: 22 of them were Jewish and had valid US visas; the remaining six—four Spanish citizens and two Cuban nationals—had valid entry documents. One further passenger, after attempting to commit suicide, was evacuated to a hospital in Havana. The remaining 908 passengers (one passenger had died of natural causes en route)—including one non-refugee, a Hungarian Jewish businessman—had been awaiting entry visas and carried only Cuban transit visas issued in Germany. Seven hundred and forty three had been waiting to receive US visas. The Cuban government refused to admit them or to allow them to disembark from the ship.

Numerous money-grubbing Cuban officials, thinking they could extort additional monies from this "rich boatload of wealthy Jews", started changing the rules of the game. The eagerly waiting passengers learned that each foreigner had to pay $500 to disembark. Pooling all the money they had, the Jews sent it ashore. However, instead of solving the problem it only whetted the appetites of those it was supposed to satiate. Suddenly it seemed that every hand was out in the Cuban bureaucracy and the smell of money in the air signaled that much more could be extracted.

Captain Schröder

Because war was looming on the horizon, the German owners of the Hamburg-America Line were afraid the MS *St. Louis* would be impounded by the allies. **Captain Gustav Schröder** was put under pressure to unload those Jews and immediately make the return run to Germany. After sitting idle for five days in the sweltering Cuban harbor, the Cuban President ordered the ship out of his waters. The captain reluctantly ordered the crew to weigh anchor. While still in Havana, he decided to make an attempt to unload his passengers in Florida or somewhere else on the East coast of the United States.

78

While waiting offshore, hoping and praying for emergency permission from the US State Department to disembark, the MS *St. Louis* passengers could see the lights of Miami. Cables sent to President Roosevelt requesting help went unanswered. However, in typically hollow State Department bureaucratize they received the following death sentence telegram stating, "... the passengers must await their turns on the waiting list and qualify for and obtain immigration visas before they may be admissible into the United States."

Unquestionably, President Roosevelt could have easily used Executive Action to grant an exception to the discriminatory regulations regarding refugees which had been imposed years before as the National Origins Quota Act of 1924. But it was for strictly political reasons that FDR refused to even consider allowing any more refugees, especially Jewish refugees, to enter the USA. Had he been motivated by any other factors than his overwhelming political calculations, he could have allowed those 900 people to enter.

The presidential election coming up in November was to be FDR's unprecedented third term. He knew that the Unions, who had great power within the Democratic party, would be unalterably opposed to allowing refugees into the country who would take American union worker's jobs. Roosevelt, being the consummate political animal, was way too wary to touch that hot wire issue, especially since his previous eight years of economic policies were showing no signs of extricating the economy from the depths of the Great Depression. In his view, those 900 Jewish refugees were just a minor blip on the radar scope of big-time politics and he rightly believed they would soon disappear as an issue.

But, where were the voices in the Christian wilderness shouting to remind their elected representatives that God had promised to curse those who ignored the plight of His Chosen People? Was Proverbs 24 not in the English Bibles of 1939? *"Rescue those being led away to death: hold back those staggering toward slaughter. If you say "But we knew nothing about this." does not He who weighs the heart perceive it? Does not He who guards your life know it? Will He not repay each person according to what he has done? "*

Evidently, the American church was either uninformed or uncaring about the MS *St. Louis* refugees. There were no protests or posters.

Indifference and politics trumped the impending disaster languishing off our eastern shore. Where was the public outrage about our government ignoring the Jewess Emma Lazarus' words, "… Give me your tired, your poor, your huddled masses yearning to breathe free, the wretched refuse of your teeming shore. Send these, the homeless, tempest-tossed to me, I lift my lamp beside the golden door!"

Tragically, it soon became apparent to the ship's captain that no permission was going to be granted and that he had no choice but to return his human cargo back to Germany. The passengers were devastated when they learned about their forced return to Germany.

The reason I am recounting this tragic incident is to give you a sense of the pressures behind the scenes boiling during that time in our history. Also, this information is to show the culpability our elected leaders had in making short-sighted but politically expedient decisions. One would hope that this 'politics only' attitude would be unfathomable to future generations, but as Democratic House Leader Tip O'Neil often opined, "All politics are local and very short-sighted."

President Roosevelt would not grant an exception to the exclusionary immigration regulations for the 900 Jewish refugees aboard the MS *St. Louis*. That June 1939, he sealed their fateful return to the charnel house of Europe. In fairness to FDR's decision, Congress had recently allowed a bill to die in committee that would have allowed 20,000 Jewish refugee children to enter the United States above the set quota. There wasn't any political will or foresight to even open Emma Lazarus' golden door, not even a crack.

Gustav Schröder, the ship's captain, became a hero in this tragedy when he insisted that his passengers be treated with respect. Even though he knew it would be viewed unfavorably by the ship's German owners and the Nazis, he allowed his passengers to conduct religious service s on board. Schröder took the lead in negotiating with Germany's European enemies such as Britain, France, Belgium, and the Netherlands. Thanks to his intervention, several countries were willing to take the refugees. They stepped up to the plate while the US quietly hid in the shadows of the dugout.

Passengers taken in by different countries:

Great Britain: 287 passengers
France: 224 (of whom 86 perished during the war),
Belgium: 214 (of whom 84 didn't survive)
Netherlands: 181 (of whom 84 were gassed in the Nazi death camps.)
In all, **only 278 of the more than 900 MS *St. Louis* passengers survived the Holocaust.**

In 1993, Yad Vashem awarded Captain Schröder the world's most prestigious designation as a "Righteous Gentile" for his heroic actions in saving Jewish lives by putting his own at risk.

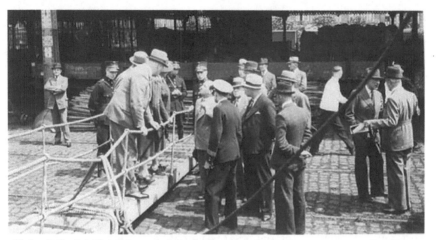

St. Louis Captain Schröder negotiates landing permits for the passengers with Belgian officials in the Port of Antwerp.

Soon after the *St. Louis* tragedy, war was declared on Nazi Germany. Schröder was assigned a desk job and never again went to sea. After the war, he worked as a writer and tried to sell his story. He was released from de-Nazification proceedings on the testimony of some of his surviving Jewish refugee passengers. Gustav Schröder died in 1959 at the age of 73.

In 1938, just before the corrupt Cuban leaders upped their greed and changed their immigration policies, a Jewish musician had entered

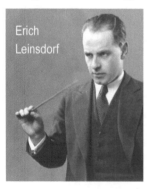

Erich Leinsdorf

Cuba. **Erich Leinsdorf** (born Erich Landauer), a world-famous Jewish-Austrian conductor, had been offered a position at the New York Metropolitan Opera, but was deported when his six-month visa had expired. Hearing about the Jewish conductor's plight, young Congressman Lyndon Johnson immediately got involved. He arranged for Leinsdorf to get his immigration status changed from "visitor" to "permanent resident" by travelling to Havana and then reentering the US under the Austrian immigration quota. Not only did Leinsdorf become a naturalized citizen in 1942, he also served in the US Armed Forces during the war.

> **"A President doesn't have a terribly long time to talk to people who are not really on the agenda."**
>
> **Erich Leinsdorf**

Both Johnson and Schröder faced the challenge of saving lives via Cuba. Without hesitation, those men rose to the occasion and did what they intuitively knew was the right thing to do even if it might have cost them their careers. In Schröder's case, by going against the will of his bosses it may even have cost him his life. Both men exhibited moral courage by taking personal and dangerous responsibility. They encountered injustice and acted.

Only five days after taking his congressional seat, Lyndon voted in favor of the Omnibus Immigration Bill which came before the House on May 18. The heart of the bill could be demonstrated by this question. "Should the United States deport or naturalize aliens - mostly Jews - from Poland and Lithuania who had entered the country illegally on false visas?" Surprisingly, the Texas Democrat broke with his beloved party and joined with most Republicans and the "Dixiecrats" of the South in voting to naturalize the illegal Jews and save them from Hitler's executioners.

In 1937, 1938 and 1939, first-term rookie congressman Lyndon Johnson was a walking-talking one man band, always tooting his own horn. His stature and his loud voice overwhelmed any room he entered; he immediately made himself the center of attention unless there was someone he wanted to court. Then he could turn on the fawning charm he was perfecting, having learned the techniques by studying politicians like his father and others. The techniques he began using during his school days were perfected while serving as Texas Congressman Kleburg's political affairs secretary.

Lyndon always stayed in contact with his good Jewish friend, Jim Novy. One day, Jim called him from Austin. "Hey, Lyndon. I'm making a trip overseas, taking my son David for his Bar Mitzvah to Palestine. But before that we are going to Poland. I want David to see where I came from and want him to meet my family members."

"Jim, you can't do that!" Lyndon exclaimed. "Hitler is going to invade Poland and kill all your Jews. I know it. I've been reading that book about him for the past ten years. You know the one I'm always talking about... that fella' Pierre van Paassen's book, *NAZISM: An Assault on Civilization.* That little Kraut Hitler will kill your family and friends unless somebody can get them out of there and bring them to Texas."

When Jim remained adamant about his plans, Lyndon said, "OK. You're going to do it, therefore I'm going to make arrangements to have visas ready in Warsaw for your family members. You've got to get them out, because they are going to be killed if you don't."
Novy responded, "Lyndon, you know as well as I do that Roosevelt is not letting any Jewish refugees into this country. How in the world can we get them exit visas?"
"You just leave that to me! Your job is to get your *Yiddishe tokhes* (Jewish posterior) over there, find your people and I'll do the rest. I can pull this off. Just don't tell Roosevelt!"

And guess what?
This still-wet-behind-the-ears congressman was able to pull it off. He called the Embassy in Warsaw and when Jim got there the visas were waiting for him. However, by the time he arrived in his hometown, some of his brothers already had been taken away and imprisoned.
Other family members, for different reasons, also couldn't get out.
However, thanks to Lyndon's help, Novy was able to rescue 42 Jews before the Nazi tanks rolled into Poland. This small but successful exploit fired up the young congressman and impelled him into even more daring adventures in attempting to rescue European Jews. Many of those schemes were undoubtably illegal and if found out, would have meant the end of his career. FDR liked him, so he needed to stay on the good side of the President, but on the other hand, he was already bending and breaking the rules whenever he thought necessary.

"Operation Texas" was Johnson and Jim Novy's undercover operation to relocate European Jews to Texas, away from Nazi persecution. Between 1938 and 1940, LBJ secretly established a refugee center in Texas for European Jews fleeing Nazi Germany. Johnson may have helped four or five hundred European Jews enter Texas through Cuba, Mexico and South America and then hid them in NYA training camps across the state. Because it was illegal to house and train non-citizens at the camps, Jim Novy reimbursed camp directors for all their costs. For decades, "Operation Texas" was kept a secret.

Money raised from political supporters bought false passports and visas in Cuba, Mexico, and other Latin American countries. The refugees entered through Galveston, which coincidentally happened to still have Adrian Levy, that Republican Jewish mayor, at the helm.

Was it really a coincidence that Lyndon just happened to know all the workings of the NYA and the location of all those camps scattered around Texas? Johnson's task was made easier because his longtime friend, Jesse Kellum, personally selected by Johnson to take his place, was then directing the NYA in Texas. In the camps, the refugees were being trained to be welders, among other things. Once the war started, the refugees that Lyndon snuck into the country (without FDR's knowledge) began working as welders in the shipyards. They helped build the ships that our Navy desperately needed.

After the Pearl Harbor attack, Johnson and several other congressmen who had been called to active duty, were summoned back to Washington by FDR who said, "No! As elected officials of the government you have to serve out your elected term."

"I'd rather give my life than be afraid to give it." LBJ

Johnson was released from active duty on July 16, 1942.

In March 1942, LBJ spoke at a fundraiser at Jim Novy's home in Austin, ostensibly to raise money for war bonds. In less than 20 minutes, the 25 people present pledged $65,000. The reporters were then asked to leave the house.

The moment they were gone, Jim, Lyndon and a number of Jewish supporters got down to the real business and a substantial sum was raised to help the Jewish underground fighters in Palestine. As a result, it was later claimed that they secretly shipped arms to Palestine in heavy crates stamped "Texas Grapefruit."

The Holocaust Revealed

In the beginning of April 1945 as the Second World War was drawing to a close, the US army 4th Armored Division approached an internment camp, Ohrdruf, near the small German town of Gotha.

One of the soldiers wrote: "About 10 miles out of town we began smelling something and we didn't know what it was. This terrible smell was indescribable. And as we got closer to town we saw people that looked like skeletons in striped pajamas, kind of wandering around on the road."

The soldiers discovered one of the German concentration camps. The prison guards had already abandoned their posts as the US Army was advancing. Bodies, dead for weeks were stacked up like cordwood and because the Germans didn't take time to burn them, the stench was indescribable. The moment General Eisenhower was informed about it, he took some his staff and sped to verify this atrocity.

Because it was so unexpected and overwhelming to his war-hardened sensibilities he initially believed that this was an anomaly and, "There just couldn't have been any other places like this hell hole." Little could Ike have imagined at the time what Holocaust horrors remained to be uncovered.

LIBERATION OF BUCHENWALD CONCENTRATION CAMP – 11 APRIL 1945

Eisenhower was known for his big smile but on this picture, there is no smile on his face – his jaw is locked. You can see he is fuming inwardly. Behind him is General George 'blood-and-guts' Patton – the toughest soldier of his time. When he walked into the camp and saw the melting stacks of bodies and smelled the stench, he turned and vomited as did many of the military staff that accompanied the generals. General Eisenhower turned around and told the photographer that accompanied him: "Get it all on the record now. Get the photos, the films, the witnesses, get it all on the record. Because somewhere down the road of history some S.O.B. will say that this never happened."

Most of the first-hand evidence that we have of these terrible crime-scene camps and what the Nazis had been doing all those years came from this first moment of Eisenhower's righteous anger. Even though the war was still going on and there was still much fighting ahead, he wanted to get as many army units in this part of Germany as possible. He wanted them to see this camp before continuing with the campaign. "People will not believe what the Nazis did."

He didn't know yet that there were hundreds of camps just like this one, throughout Germany. Neither did he yet know about the Polish extermination camps, such as Auschwitz and Birkenau where the killings mounted into the millions.

Ike was so moved by what he saw that he wanted the world to know what happened in the concentration camps. He cabled General Marshall, the head of the Chief of Staff of the United States Army with a request to bring members of Congress and journalists to the newly discovered camps in Germany so that they would bring the horrible truth about Nazi atrocities to the American public.

Perhaps this is one of the reasons that God later blessed Eisenhower with the presidency from 1953-1961 Eventually, exposing these atrocities to the world became a blessing to the Jewish people. After seeing those terrible pictures, many people swore the oath, "This will never, ever happen again!"

When Lyndon heard about the camps, he joined a group of congressmen that visited Dachau and first hand witnessed what had happened to the Jews.

Lady Bird wrote, "When Lyndon returned home, he was still shaken from what he saw. He was stunned, terrorized, bursting with an overpowering revulsion and incredulous horror at what he had seen. He always had this openness toward Jews but even more after that unforgettable experience."

Johnson had an almost mystical belief about his powers of persuasion. Even as a child he believed that if he could get right into your face and stare intently into your eyes, he could change your mind on anything. Being taller than most people he would get right up into and above their face if he wanted them to do something. He would do this to friends and enemies alike. I'm certain that sometimes Lyndon would eat garlic on purpose before getting in the person's face so that they would want to get over the 'friendly persuasion' as soon as possible. This was a technique he started to develop even in high school when he ran for class president. He was perfecting the "Johnson treatment" as he became a Congressman and then Senator. Using the aforementioned technique, he became the most powerful and persuasive majority leader to ever dominate the Senate. Nothing moved through the Senate without Lyndon's approval. He loved power. The only next powerful position would have been the presidency and that desire always burned in his heart. He always dreamed and schemed toward grabbing that ring.

Kennedy Beats Lyndon to the Draw
and Then Makes an Offer

"Landslide Lyndon" won the Texas Democratic primary by 87 "suspicious" votes in 1948 and immediately set to work to become the Senate Majority Leader, the next rung on the ladder to the top.
In the late '50's he actually decided that he was going to run for president in 1960. A possible opponent whom he disdained as a "do-nothing back-bencher" and a rich playboy was "Massachusetts Handsome Jack." In 1953, John F. Kennedy was elected as the Junior Senator from Massachusetts, but he hardly ever showed up for work.

1948 Senate Campaign

89

Lyndon was sure that his own work ethic and desire to be president would culminate in the 1960 election. After much soul-searching and worry over an early death or worse, an election defeat, he finally judged that the time was right, and he was going to throw his Stetson into the ring. However, this fearful cowboy was hesitant to pull the trigger.

Because he kept holding back, at the last moment Kennedy beat him to the draw and Handsome Jack announced he was going to run. Even though Johnson made a last-gasp attempt, it was too little and too late - JFK easily wrapped up the nomination.

Believing that all Johnson men were destined to die young, Johnson had a clock ticking in his head. This explains what drove him to accomplish so much in such a short time and the reason why he put in 18-20-hour work days and demanded the same from his staff. He now sadly realized that his on-again off-again hesitancy to run got him beat by this handsome youngster. Realizing he was getting older and uglier, Lyndon was about to crawl into bed and pull the covers over his head again.

Just when it seemed the darkest night of his life, things suddenly changed when Kennedy sent him a note offering the Vice Presidency. Johnson didn't know how to respond. He had some powerful political

godfathers from Texas, Sam Rayburn and 'Cactus' Jack Garner, who had been Vice president under FDR. Jack Garner had been the Speaker of the House, which is as far as you can get on top of the dog pile called Congress. So, when FDR asked Garner to be Vice president , he took it.

Then, for two too long administrations he was the VP who did absolutely nothing and lost all of his power. Nobody

Senator Johnson and Speaker Sam Rayburn feared "Cactus Jack" anymore, nobody cared what he said. He was the one who quoted, "Being VP was like a bucket of warm spit." He had been worthless!

And now Johnson was offered that same Vice Presidency but could not make up his mind. "Should I take it or not? I'd be just a heartbeat away from being the president. But I've seen what it did to old Cactus Jack – that nothing job just drained all the life out of him.

When FDR was finished with him, he just threw him out on his ear.

"Would Jack Kennedy do that to me? No, but that mean little brother Bobby, would if he had half a chance."

For a very long time, that day at the Democratic convention, Lyndon worried back and forth over this offer.

Finally, he gave his answer. "Yes. I'll do it."

Kennedy, the stereotypical liberal Northeasterner knew he needed the Southern vote. Even though Lyndon was a different breed of cat from Texas, the southerners felt that underneath those chaps he was undoubtedly one of their guys and he could be counted on to oppose all that civil rights stuff.

Kennedy needed him and treated him with respect, but **Bobby,** the dark prince and his courtiers fervently hated Johnson. Behind his back they called him "Colonel Cornpone" and snickered at cracks about his "hound dog ears and eyes" and not always behind his back.

The respect and fear which Johnson had grown accustomed to as the powerful Majority Leader of the Senate was now totally absent in the White House and also back in his home state.

This 'power failure' affected Johnson greatly during the next two years as VP. It took all the pizzazz out of him. The guy that used to be big and loud and robust became quiet, morose and sullen.

> **"Jack was out kissing babies while I was out passing bills. Someone had to tend the store." LBJ**

He would sit in meetings without saying a word and looked like a tired old beagle that just lost his best friend. He came early in the morning and sat in the office of the president's secretary, hoping to catch the president's eye, hoping against hope that JFK might wave at him and invite him in for a few minutes.

Most of the time he had to go back to his lonely, quiet place in the old Executive Office Building and just squat there with nothing to do. For an antsy, driven, constantly in motion man, this was the ultimate punishment - nothing to do. He felt that his very lifeblood was being drained out of his arteries. Life was slowly oozing out of his limp wrists. It was a very tough time for Lyndon Johnson.

He was quoted about his empty time in the empty office of the Vice president by writing,

> **"To hunger for use and to go unused is the worst hunger of all."**

We don't know how many times Lyndon talked about a special verse but he used to quote one Bible verse quite often. He'd say, "Now, let us reason together" (Isaiah 1:18). There was a spiritual side to Lyndon that hardly anyone knew about. But it must have been during dry times like this that the still and persistent voice of his Aunt Jessie bubbled to the surface with encouraging scriptures like,

"So do not throw away your confidence; it will be richly rewarded. You need to persevere so that when you have done the will of God you will receive what he has promised."
Hebrews 10:35-36.

But now he was slowly losing his confidence as his power drained away. He realized that nobody feared him anymore. He was becoming a replica of other do-nothing VPs and then he heard the rumor that Kennedy was not going to have him as his vice president during the next election.

Lyndon's life for the previous 30 years had been mostly lived in Washington with short visits back home. As vice president , he no longer even had a state office in Texas.

The political power base in Texas had moved on without him and he had a sixth sense about keeping or losing power like no one else ever had. He knew he had lost it back home and in DC.

JFK kept nudging Lyndon to set up a fund-raising and fence-mending gala trip to Texas for him and Jackie. He reminded Lyndon that he had a major debt to pay off before the next upcoming election and he would need a lot of that Texas oil money. Lyndon kept avoiding setting a date for the affair because he knew JFK was not very popular in Texas and he also knew that his own popularity had hit the skids. Lyndon was also hearing the rumors that JFK was considering dumping him from the ticket that coming Fall. Finally, the president forced Lyndon into a corner for the Texas fundraisers and he reluctantly complied with making the arrangements. The plan was to fly to San Antonio and then to Houston and up to Fort Worth in the evening on Thursday, the 21st of November. The next two events were a luncheon in Dallas and a dinner in Austin.

Johnson, Texas Governor John Connally and Senator Ralph Yarborough all arrived on the vice president 's plane in Fort Worth. However, Yarborough couldn't stand either one of them and he was unwilling to travel in the same car as Johnson, who was a lifetime friend of his former aide John Connally. After much embarrassing jockeying for position in the vehicles at Fort Worth, which was mentioned in the morning papers, the president bluntly told Yarborough he had to ride with the VP and that the Governor would ride with him and the First Lady.

The day of infamy, Friday the 22nd of November 1963, started as an overcast and rainy morning in Fort Worth. The day's events began with an outdoor address in the rain by the president and a Chamber of Commerce Breakfast at the Hotel Texas, followed by an extremely short flight to Love Field and a caravan to downtown Dallas for a luncheon.

"I seldom think of politics more than eighteen hours a day." LBJ

Because of protocol the Vice president never flew on Air Force One, so Lyndon had to hurry to every airport ahead of the president and first lady. He had to wait for them in San Antonio, at the bottom of the steps and say something like, "Welcome to Texas Mr. President and Mrs. Kennedy, come on down. Welcome to my state." It wasn't his state anymore. As a matter of fact his protégée, John Connally, was now the governor and the new big deal in the Lone Star State.

Then Lyndon had to hurry ahead to Houston and Fort Worth and stand there again and go through the same charade of welcoming the president. Lyndon hoped to get into the president's car but no, the governor was riding with the president, that vehicle was followed by four motorcycles and the next car was the Secret Service vehicle. The Johnsons were stuck with the very unhappy Senator Yarborough at quite a distance back in the cavalcade of cars.

Texas senator Ralph Yarbrough (3rd from the right, next to John Connally) listens a speech in Fort Worth during Kennedy's trip to Texas. The media reported that Yarborough refused to ride in the same car as Johnson in a motorcade, and LBJ commented that the "newspaper boys went wild."

This was possibly one of the worst days of LBJ's life. He had feared that he had no respect or prospects left anywhere in politics (which was all he knew or cared about).

He couldn't even get a good car seat through his own state.

As the limousines were moving slowly through the downtown canyons he could hear the screaming of the people for Jackie and JFK. Can't you just imagine the screams, cheers and whistles of the crowd on the sidewalk as Jack and Jackie smiled and waved. Their attention seemed to pull the people along in the car's wake. By the time Lyndon's car arrived, the streets were mostly deserted and silent.

He was shocked to realize that there were no cheering crowds left to pay homage to an old powerless has-been. This latest snub must have overtaxed Johnson's broken heart as the truth revealed the unbearably bitter fact that life for him was effectively over. He now knew for sure as he gazed at the empty sidewalks that he was never going to be president, nor even a second shot at that 'bucket of warm spit.' He must have been wishing that he could disappear into his bed and pull the covers over his head and never come out.

As he stared at the carpet on the floor of the steel grey 1964 Lincoln convertible he and Bird were seated in, something got his attention and broke his slide into depression. At first, he thought it was firecrackers, but within seconds he was jumped upon and pinned to the floor by Rufus Youngblood, a giant of a Secret Service man. The car leaped ahead and careened out of Dealey Plaza and raced toward Parkland Hospital. No one in the car really knew what had happened other than shots had been fired. The high-speed 8-minute race to the hospital didn't provide any further information as to what had occurred.

As soon as the car screeched to a halt, the Johnsons were roughly hustled into an empty hospital room and kept out of sight and under protection. While Lyndon and Lady Bird waited there they were ignored because they were not part of the Kennedy 'team'. No one would tell them anything, especially not a prognosis as to whether or not JFK was going to live or die. The confused and deflated VP stood there with a blank look on his big face, again feeling the pain of being kept out of the information loop because he was "Colonel Cornpone" and not a citizen of Camelot.

The assistant White House Press Secretary **Malcolm Kilduff** (with cigarette) received the terrible news from the surgeons that the president was dead! He was told to give the news to Johnson. Kilduff, only an assistant, didn't have the experience, courage or the words to carry such a heavy historical message. As he nervously approached the gaunt and formidable vice president he was struggling for just the right combination of words for this message. He stammered and cleared his throat and started and finished with, "Mr. President."
It was enough. Message received! That two-word title signaled that the LBJ story was not over yet by a long shot.

Johnson seemed to immediately grasp the gravity of the times and the position that he had longed for all his life but had become convinced he would never get. Close observers have said that Lyndon started growing in wisdom and stature almost immediately and during the next few days, the transformation was absolutely incredible.
The new President of the United States wasn't that gruff, loud, crude talking tough guy, because his first question was, "What about Mrs. Kennedy?" He also realized that this attack could be much more widespread and might even be focused on all the leaders of the government.

His immediate vision was wide and far-reaching while that of the Kennedy staff was bitter, hurt, limited and mean - at least for the moment. The Kennedy "Irish Mafia" did not want Lyndon to set even a foot onto "Kennedy's" Air Force One. They didn't want Mrs. Kennedy or the president's body on the same plane with Lyndon.

With guns drawn by the Secret Service , the staff "confiscated" the body from the Dallas hospital in order to prevent the county coroner from doing an autopsy as required by Texas law.

The Johnsons were rushed back to Love Field where they boarded Air Force One (the one he was never allowed on before) and then began considering all the details to be taken care of before they could leave.

Presidents had always been sworn-in at the Capitol, but could or should it be done while still in Dallas?

In an extraordinary phone call, LBJ phoned the Attorney General for an opinion. The extraordinary part is that the AG was his nemesis Bobby Kennedy. Bobby was unable to respond and said he would "Get back to you on that."

Johnson was advised to return to DC immediately. Johnson said he would not leave without Jackie Kennedy, and she had let it be known that she would not leave without her husband's body.

At that time, he was the de facto president but the Kennedy people didn't want him to be on THAT plane.

There was a delay in getting both Mrs. Kennedy and the casket to the airfield and on the plane. Of course, Jackie was in shock and others were pressing Johnson to be quickly sworn-in.

However, Lyndon had something else in mind. When he was VP he tried to appoint Sarah Hughes of Dallas to a federal judgeship. He suspected that her appointment had been blocked by Bobby to intentionally snub him. "Before anybody swears me in," Johnson said, "I need to have the exact wording of the oath and you've got to find Judge Hughes for me— she's going to do the oath."

In the meantime, the oath was typed out and ready for the missing judge to appear.

Aides calling the office of Judge Sarah T. Hughes were told she was out of the office. The new president called back and barked, "This is Lyndon Johnson. Find her!"

And find her they did, but it wasn't easy. Her staff and the police and Secret Service and the FBI were all alerted to find her. She had been at the Trade Mart waiting for the president to come to the luncheon that never happened. Following the news of the shooting, the attendees had scattered. Finally, she was located and whisked out to Love Field. The diminutive lady clambered up the stairs of Air Force One and breathlessly and solemnly administered the oath. Lyndon added his own touch to the oath by "swearing" (not affirming) and adding, "So help me God!"

> *"I do solemnly swear (or affirm) that I will faithfully execute the office of president of the United States, and will to the best of my ability, preserve, protect and defend the Constitution of the United States."*

The photo on the next page is one of the most famous pictures of the decade: Judge Hughes is hardly in the picture because she was such a tiny woman and Lyndon was such an overpowering big man that the photographer could barely fit them into the cramped space of the plane. You can see Lady Bird Johnson is in the picture, under Lyndon's right hand as he swears the oath: he made sure that Jackie Kennedy was right next to him. The man in the left corner holding the mike is Malcolm Kilduff, the Press Officer.

The plane's engines started during the swearing in and the plane was airborne in minutes.

When Air Force One landed at Andrews AFB in Washington at 6:10 PM the new president solemnly walked to a bank of microphones and spoke briefly to the nation, "This is a sad time for all people. We have suffered a loss that cannot be weighed. For me, it is a deep personal tragedy. I know that the world shares the sorrow that Mrs. Kennedy and her family bear. I will do my best. That is all I can do. I ask for your help — and God's."

On the way to the vice president's home his mind was going 100 miles an hour. When he got home some of his key staff were already there. He worked most of the night. He realized that he couldn't rush into the White House. He said, "I can't move in and take it over. It is still Jackie's home and all the rest of it and we are not going to sweep her out of there, as had happened sometimes with other presidents when they had to leave and kind of left with a bad taste in their mouths." That night Johnson sat at home with his team and spent at least five hours mapping out what would become his Great Society agenda for the next six years.

He met the Israeli Ambassador and spoke with a kindness and a reassuring tone, "You've lost a very great friend (meaning Jack Kennedy)". And then he said something unexpected, "But, you found an even better one!"

And that is exactly what happened. Over the years, they found that Lyndon Johnson, was a better friend to Israel than President Kennedy had been or would have been had he lived.

After all this, the question remains:

How did God use Lyndon Johnson in the White House?

Look at this Scripture and make note of it. Maybe you've had a desire in your heart. Maybe you believe for something. Maybe it's been years, whatever it is, and it doesn't seem to come to pass and you're losing your confidence that it's going to happen. You find yourself saying, "Well, I guess that I misunderstood. God really doesn't want me to do this stuff." Don't throw away your confidence!

Hebrews 10:35. "So do not throw away your confidence; it will be richly rewarded. You need to persevere so that when you have done the will of God, you will receive what He has promised."

You need to persevere. Push on! Stay with it! So, when you've done the will of God, you will receive what He has promised.

> **"I will do my best. That is all I can do. I ask for your help - and God's." LBJ**
>
> **"I'm the only president you've got."**

While serving as president, Johnson spent an inordinate amount of time at the ranch house in Stonewall. The house was small and his office was about 12' by 12'. In that tiny office there was just room for him, a picture of a beagle on the wall and a little place for his secretary.

When the Cabinet and Joint Chiefs of Staff would come to meet with him they all couldn't fit into his tiny office. Instead, they would meet outside under a giant oak tree. It certainly was a different kind of a presidency.

He knew quite a bit about the Bible. Many people think, "Ah, well, he was just a politician and didn't care much about that Bible stuff."

As usual with LBJ, there was another side to him that most people didn't know about. Sometimes on Sunday, there was a spiritual yearning that came out in very unusual ways. Occasionally he'd go to two or three churches, not to be seen going there, but he was after something. He had his own church in Washington and his own pastor there but that wasn't enough to satisfy some longing he had for more. He 'adopted' a little Catholic priest from Stonewall, Texas. As soon as he would fly into the ranch he'd say, "Where is that priest at?" And when the priest would come out he'd say, "Hey, we're going to Germany. Get your toothbrush, come with us."

Billy Graham wrote in his book about his memories of his time with Lyndon Johnson. There would be times that Lyndon would say, "Get in the car, preacher." And they'd drive out in his convertible across the

ranch and he'd park under some trees, get out, then throw himself on the ground, saying "Pray for me, preacher!"

That's not usually what you think about Lyndon Johnson or any president. God had him there for this reason.

Of the many wars Israel has been involved in, the one in June of 1967 was probably the most significant war in the history of the young nation. It is known as the Six-Day War.

The Arab attack was preempted by Israel attacking the armies of Egypt and Syria which were lining up to start attacking Israel. One of the telling conversations that was taped on the phone and transcribed was Lyndon Johnson speaking to the Prime Minister of Israel, Levi Eshkol, before the fighting started. Those Arab armies were primed to wreak revenge on Israel for the defeats and embarrassment the Israelis had visited upon them during the 1948 Arab-Israeli war. Egypt under Nasser was broadcasting that they were going to run all the Jews into the ocean. The Syrians and the Jordanians echoed the threats and joined together in a unified command to put an ignominious end to the Zionist entity. It was just a matter of hours or days until the slaughter would commence.

P.M. Levy Eshkol, commander of Honor Guard Col. Conmy, president Lyndon Johson inspecting the guard of Honor in Washington, 1964.

In 1967 the US armed forces were deeply committed in the quagmire called Viet Nam. Militarily, there was little the United States could do to help defend Israel.

In the phone conversation between Johnson and the Israeli PM, Johnson is heard to say in his deepest Texas drawl, "Now listen, Mister Prime Minister. You let them draw first. You let them draw and shoot first and then we can jump in there and help you out..."

In every cowboy movie Lyndon ever saw, the bad guy in the black hat got to draw first in the iconic gun fight and then the guy in the white hat could plug him.

102

In that order there's no problem because the bad guy tried to commit murder and the good guy was only acting in self-defense. He saw most things in that sort of light. "You let them hit you first!" he thundered definitively.

The PM of Israel was not going to preside over the second Holocaust. He was not going to let them do it, so as Lyndon hung up the phone, he looked at an aide and said, "I know damn well that Israel's going to hit them first."

And that is exactly what Israel did. That momentous event is called the Six-Day War. In many ways it was during the first six hours that the fate of Egypt and Syria was already settled. Israel's preemptive strike on their airfields wiped out hundreds of fighter planes and the new MIGs that the Russians had supplied them with. The Arab armor and infantry had no air cover for their thousands of tanks that were already on the move heading toward Israel. Of course, there was terrible fighting on the ground, it wasn't a cake walk by any means. But within a few days that war was over, and Israel had gained almost 3 times the land they had previously. Most importantly, they reunited the city of Jerusalem. It was the first time in over 2500 years that Jews were in charge of their own Jewish capital, the old city of Jerusalem. These are the famous pictures of this Jewish army reaching the Western Wall/Wailing Wall for prayer. Rabbi **Shlomo Goren,** the Chief Rabbi of the army, is shown blowing the shofar. That was the first time that had happened in many centuries. Jews had been banned from even getting near that wall for 19 years since the Jordanians had taken over the city in 1948.

But Jesus warned us that:
"Jerusalem will be trampled on by the Gentiles until the times of the Gentiles are fulfilled." Luke 21:24. NIV

That startling and lightning-fast war happened while LBJ was in office. The euphoric celebration throughout Israel, the opening of the plaza in front of the Wailing Wall and thousands arriving for prayer at the wall was a historic and tremendous moment. The original city of Jerusalem, after 2500 years, came back into the hands of the Jewish people. The city of Jerusalem was no longer being administered by Gentile rulers and it was not being trodden down by the Gentiles any more. As soon as the actual fighting in the field had finished, the real battle to strip Israel of the victory began at the United Nations.

For the next six months, there was incredible in-fighting at the UN to make Israel give back all the land that they had captured in their defensive war against the armies of Egypt, Syria, Jordan, etc. The overwhelming belief at the UN was that everything Israel had gained must be given back to the aggressors.

Prior to this short unexpected war something out of the ordinary took place. A life-time appointed Justice of the Supreme Court resigned his  seat. That unusual resignation was not because of age or health, the usual reasons for leaving the court. **Arthur Goldberg** was appointed to the Supreme Court by Kennedy in 1962. He was the same age as Johnson. He was the youngest of eight children from a very poor immigrant Jewish family on the west side of Chicago. He went to a Chicago city college and DePaul, not to Harvard or Yale. He cut his legal teeth defending labor unions and strikers - hardly the education or the Manhattan law firm connections that would predict a fast track to the Federal courts. But JFK appointed him to the highest court in the land in 1962. It truly was 'a rags to riches' story. It appeared that Arthur Goldberg was set for a lifetime of jurisprudence in a seat that was the envy of any lawyer in the profession.

104

In July of 1965, Adlai Stevenson, the United States Ambassador to the United Nations and former two-time Democratic Presidential candidate and Illinois Governor, suddenly died of a heart attack. Goldberg flew to the funeral on Air Force One with Johnson. It was on that flight that the president began his campaign to persuade Goldberg to resign from the court and take the UN position. LBJ must have unveiled the full frontal 'Johnson Treatment' — his special concoction of arm-twisting tactics described as a potent mixture of persuasion, badgering, flattery, threats, reminders of past favors and future advantages. Lyndon always believed if he could just get right into the face of his target and look deeply into his prey's eyes... it would soon be all over and he would get his way.

Many articles have been written trying to decipher LBJ's reasons for singling out Goldberg and opening an appointment on the court. Like most things Lyndon did, there were probably a variety of motives for his chess moves. But the point is that Arthur Goldberg was exactly the right person for the upcoming task at the UN that no one knew was going to happen in the summer of 1967. The pieces were being moved into place that still are protecting Israel today.

United Nations Resolution 242

The reason Goldberg was there was because of UN Resolution 242. That resolution would have taken all the captured land away from Israel. If passed in the Security Council the whole war, blood and treasure expended would have been for naught.

It all hinged on one tiny three-letter article: 'THE'. Arthur Goldberg was able to change it all by arguing for the exclusion of 'the'.

Johnson talked to Goldberg on the phone (I've read the transcripts) "We're not gonna go all limp tail on little Israel. You gotta do everything you can – we're going to back them as much as we possibly can."

In the UN, Goldberg was closely collaborating with Johnson on the smallest of words in the text of the resolution and holding out against most all the other nations of the world. After weeks of debate and heated arguments it all came down to that pesky article, 'THE'.

The ORIGINAL TEXT read:

"…withdrawal of Israel armed forces from THE TERRITORIES occupied in the recent conflict."

Goldberg, the master wordsmith had deleted 'the', it changed the resolution entirely.

The FINAL TEXT read:

"Withdrawal of Israel armed forces from TERRITORIES occupied in the recent conflict." ('the' removed).

The word 'territories' meant the West Bank, the Sinai, the Golan Heights, and the Old City of Jerusalem. The fight to modify the resolution went on for nearly five months until Goldberg got 'THE' removed from the resolution.

This now means that Israel can remove themselves from all the territories – some of the territories or none of them. All territorial changes now have to be settled by negotiations and actually sitting down and legally recognizing the various enemies. That minor (but truly major) change still holds today.

More than 50 years later that resolution has been recognized as international law and is still applicable to any settlement between the warring parties. Israel does not have to involuntarily give up any of that captured land unless they agree to a negotiated settlement.

Certainly, the United States and most other countries have tried to shame, pressure, coerce, or force Israel to give up those hard won gains. However, Johnson was responsible for getting Goldberg off the Supreme Court and into the UN, pressuring and pushing and it became one of the great advances between the US and Israel.

Soviet Premier Kosygin asked Johnson, "Why are you supporting Israel? There are only 3 million Jews when there are 80 million Arabs?"

Johnson responded, "Because it's the right thing to do!"

Lyndon Baines Johnson became a blessing to Israel and he strengthened the US-Israel relationship to a whole new level. Lyndon Johnson was a man that God put in the Oval Office of the White House for the purpose of bringing a blessing to the Jewish People and the Jewish Land.

107

And it's true: Israel did find a better friend when God put Johnson into the White House for that purpose and for that moment in time.

Was LBJ Jewish?

The following was published in *The 5 Towns Jewish Times* on 11 April 2013:

Lyndon Johnson's maternal ancestors, the Huffmans, apparently migrated to Frederick, Maryland from Germany sometime in the mid-eighteenth century. Later they moved to Bourbon, Kentucky and eventually settled in Texas in the mid-to-late nineteenth century.

According to Jewish law, if a person's mother is Jewish, then that person is automatically Jewish, regardless of the father's ethnicity or religion. The facts indicate that both of Lyndon Johnson's great-grandparents, on the maternal side, were Jewish.

These were the grandparents of Lyndon's mother, Rebecca Baines. Their names were John S. Huffman and Mary Elizabeth Perrin. John Huffman's mother was Suzanne Ament, a common Jewish name. Perrin is also a common Jewish name.

Huffman and Perrin had a daughter, Ruth Ament Huffman, who married Joseph Baines and together they had a daughter, Rebekah Baines, Lyndon Johnson's mother. The line of Jewish mothers can be traced back three generations in Lyndon Johnson's family tree. There is little doubt that Lyndon was our first Jewish President!.

Aunt Jessie Hatcher

We're studying about a president who had little seeds planted early in his head and heart. We know that his mother did a lot of this. She really thought that Lyndon Johnson was going to turn into something outstanding and she pushed him in that direction with her own elocution lessons. He didn't get that approbation from his daddy, but the one woman who hovered over him all of his life was his Aunt Jessie Johnson Hatcher. She always seemed to be there in times of his need when he was young. She helped him with tuition through college. He lived at her house when he was teaching high school in Houston.

She always had an open invitation to be at the ranch when he'd come back from DC. After he won a landslide election in 1964, the only time he ran for president, a reporter interviewing Aunt Jessie said,

"So of course you voted for your nephew, but I want to ask you --- " Aunt Jessie stopped him in mid-sentence, "Now, hold it right there! I didn't vote for him. As a matter of fact, I never vote. I always vote for Jesus, that's what I do."

She would always bring these conversations around to her beliefs. And her major belief was, not only that Jesus was a Jew, but that all the Jews today are Abraham's descendants and how we have to be a blessing to them. And that's always what she would say to Lyndon, from the time he was a young boy, all through his presidency.

Every time he'd come back and see Aunt Jessie, the first question was, "Lyndon, what have you done for the Jews?"

Lyndon did a lot for the Jews in those days but it was always his Aunt Jessie who reminded him of his responsibility to the Jews and she was a regular at the ranch. The ranch house wasn't a glamorous, multi-million dollar home, but just an old ranch house painted up on the Pedernales. In the cramped dining room, LBJ's seat was at the head of a long table. He had a telephone screwed right into the leg of the table, so he could always be talking. In his line of sight, out on the porch, he had three TV's individually tuned to ABC, CBS and NBC. Because there was no such thing as a remote control, he had them all on at once. By looking over the heads of his guests he could monitor those screens. Aunt Jessie was usually at the table with him.

Once he had Konrad Adenauer (the Chancellor of West German) sitting across from Aunt Jessie. Johnson said, "Now, Aunt Jessie. Do you have anything you'd like to ask the Chancellor of Germany?" He sat back with a big smile on his face, because he knew the coming question.

Leaning across that table, Aunt Jessie said, "What are you doing for the Jews lately?"

That was her theme in life. She never let Lyndon get away from that.

All of his life she was there. Even at his funeral she was there. He is buried right across the road from the little house where he was born 64 years earlier.

He once told Mrs. Johnson, "When I die I don't just want our friends who can come in their private planes. I want the men in their pickup trucks and the women whose slips hang down below their dresses to be welcome, too...." Hundreds of people attended the funeral, which was conducted by Reverend Billy Graham. On January 25, 1973, Lyndon Johnson was laid to rest in the Johnson Family Cemetery on the LBJ Ranch. Reverend Billy Graham said,

"Here amidst these familiar hills and under these expansive skies and under these beautiful oak trees he loved so much, his earthly life has come a full circle."

God had Aunt Jessie there for a reason: to shepherd this great big boisterous politician to bless the Jews. Make no bones about it. If you read about Johnson, about his private life, he had big faults, but he also had some big wonderful things about him. I believe that all of this goes into understanding what the man was all about. God knows what's in people's hearts, and He changes things. In Scripture it says that God can move the heart of a  king like a watercourse and make it go where He wants it to go.

The story of the emperor who had no clothes illustrates the fact that those in power are often surrounded by sycophants who will flatter and pander the leader so that they can remain in the inner circle. The powerful one is shielded from scrutiny by a phalanx of public relations illusionists working around the clock covering up or spinning stories so that the missing clothes are never noticed.

In retrospect, when we are enabled to better see the entirety of a leader's life like Johnson's, we often gasp at the falsehoods surrounding the real man and despair of understanding how someone like that could have been part of a plan that God devised.

Our "Sunday School" one-dimensional flat flannel-graph expectations of whom God would select to do great things just doesn't compute when we get a glimpse or two of the unclothed emperor.

However, when we start searching the Scriptures and see the "flaws" in the lives of those individuals that God definitely chooses for His own reasons, it becomes glaringly apparent that, "His Ways are not our ways."

I find it so enlightening that the items that PR specialists would have erased from the documentary are included in the God-breathed accounts of the leaders chosen to rescue Israel. The great King David was not only an adulterer but a murderer willing to cover up his "little indiscretion with Bathsheba." Solomon, remembered as the wisest man on earth did the stupidest and most tragic things by ushering into his kingdom the false gods of his many foreign wives.

The Scriptures are full of God-chosen leaders who were fatally flawed in many ways but who rose to the occasion and were used by God to be a part of His overall plan. If you care to test this theory look for the flaws that the Bible highlights in the lives of these heroes such as Gideon, Barak, Samson, Jephthah, etc. Instead of dwelling on the "sins" that particularly upset our current moral scale, let us search for the events and character strengths that the "unseen Hand of God" was always moving and positioning.

LBJ is definitely one of these characters, fatally flawed (in retrospect) but positioned by God to be in the right place and at the opportune time and against all odds would make the right choices. Choices that others, better prepared, would not have made.

"There are no favorites in my office. I treat them all with the same general inconsideration." LBJ

LBJ with Abba Eban

LBJ had a unique and unusual relationship with God's Chosen people, the Jews.

He also had a great deal of respect for many Jewish individuals, but particularly when it came to the state of Israel.

The object of our investigation is to look for the evidence of how God was invisibly maneuvering events so Lyndon could be in place to make the critical choices that were his assignment in the grand tapestry of God's Design. Who were the "righteous enablers" who kept LBJ on the straight and narrow? Actually he strayed quite often from that path on his way to the corral all those years when he was struggling with all his might for political and personal power.

However, like any Texas Longhorn bull, there were enough drovers who could keep him mostly under control and headed in the right direction. The most influential of those drovers was his Aunt Jessie, the daughter of a cowboy who was legendary for driving herds on the Chisolm trail.

She was an "outrider" who always kept pushing, nudging and reminding Lyndon that his positions in life were given to him so that he could honor and help the Jews.

It was two weeks to the day from Lyndon's burial that 88 year old Aunt Jesse passed away from the cold and pneumonia she caught at the cemetery. It's as if she knew her work here was done!

"There are no problems we cannot solve together, and very few that we can solve by ourselves." LBJ

Johnson's Legacy for Israel

Johnson's policies stemmed mostly from personal concerns – Johnson's friendship with leading Zionists, his belief that America had a moral obligation to bolster Israel's security and his conception of Israel as a frontier land much like his home state of Texas. His personal concerns led him to intervene when he felt that the State or Defense departments had insufficiently appreciated Israel's diplomatic or military needs.

President Johnson firmly pointed American policy in a pro-Israel direction. In a historical context, the American emergency airlift to Israel in 1973, the constant diplomatic support, the economic and military assistance, the relocation of the US Embassy to Jerusalem in 2018 and the strategic bonds between the two countries can all be linked to the seeds planted by LBJ.

In Clinton Rossiter's words, "a breeding ground of indestructible myth."

Not since Andrew Jackson had a president contained such an abundance of both virtue and flaw.

1931 school debate team

"If two men agree on everything, you may be sure that one of them is doing the thinking."LBJ

TIMELINE Lyndon Johnson

1908 - Born

1927 - Graduated from college

1928 - Principal and teacher in Texas

1934 - Gets married

1937 - Elected congressman from Texas

1949 - Elected Senator

1961 - Vice president with JFK

1963 - President after JFK assassinated

1964 - Elected President for second term

1969 - Retired as President, succeeded by
       Richard Nixon

1973 - Dies at LBJ Ranch

1964 - Levi Eshkol visiting the White House

"If one morning I walked on top of the water across the Potomac River, the headline that afternoon would read: 'President Can't Swim.'"

"When I was a boy we didn't wake up with Vietnam and have Cyprus for lunch and the Congo for dinner."

"I'm tired. I'm tired of feeling rejected by the American people. I'm tired of waking up in the middle of the night worrying about the war."

"When the burdens of the presidency seem unusually heavy, I always remind myself it could be worse. I could be a mayor."

"A man without a vote is a man without protection."

PART 3

RICHARD NIXON

Richard Milhous Nixon (1913 - 1994)

Richard Milhous Nixon was the 37th president of the USA who served from   1969 – 1974. Before that he was a Senator in California and Member of the U.S. House of Representatives. Vice president under Dwight D. Eisenhower (1953-1961). Nixon was the only president to resign. He was succeeded by Gerald Ford.

INTRODUCTION

The two people previously written about were among the most unlikely candidates to ever become president. That is the uniqueness of the presidents we discuss in this book. I think it is God's way of showing that He really is in charge and does the impossible; it also shows His loving sense of humor.

In Part One we wrote that Harry Truman never wanted to be president. However, because God wanted him in that position, that's exactly where, how, when and why he ended up in the Oval Office.

Part Two was about Lyndon Johnson, who wanted that job with all his heart; his whole life he worked and schemed toward that goal. The day he became president began as the worst day of his life. It seemed all his future hopes and political power were gone. He saw the handwriting on the wall: convinced that Kennedy was dumping him from the ticket, he soon would be out of a job. With a single shot, his world changed in a heartbeat. Three and a half years later he was in the White House when the Six-Day War broke out. The things LBJ did in the war's aftermath most likely wouldn't have been done by JFK and our level of support for Israel would not be like it is today.

The next man we study was another most unlikely figure to be president. He was a presidential candidate and vice president in the Eisenhower administration, but when he campaigned for the presidency, he was narrowly beaten by John F. Kennedy. Upon returning to California, his home state, he could not get elected as governor or even dogcatcher. Most notably, he wrote what he thought to be his personal political epitaph during his 'last' press conference in which he lambasted the journalists by saying, "You won't have Dick Nixon to kick around anymore – I'm through with politics."

> **"Finishing second in the Olympics gets you silver. Finishing second in politics gets you oblivion." Nixon**

And yet, a few years later, he was elected president of the USA.

So, What Does That Have to do With Israel?
What Important Role did Nixon play in Connection to That Promised Land and the Chosen People?

Richard Nixon was an extremely complicated individual. The more you study him the more sides of his multi-faceted personality emerge.

While politicians are usually outgoing people who want to meet with other people, Nixon was withdrawn. The fact that he felt uncomfortable in crowds was especially evident during press conferences where he constantly cleared his throat and sweated profusely.

Why does he put himself through that torture if he is so uncomfortable standing in front of those hostile reporters? I used to wonder.

Nixon had a dark side when it came to the Jewish people. No one (except him) knew that everything said in the Oval Office was secretly recorded. Listening to those tapes, you hear him say the nastiest and crudest things. It sounds like most agreed with what he said - he was the president after all - and few visitors would dare contradict or disagree with the most powerful elected person in the world.

The transcripts of his remarks about the Jews implied that he was the biggest anti-Semite ever to enter the Oval Office.

Being a 'total' politician, everything was politics to Nixon. When he spoke of "Jews", he almost consistently referred to the liberal Democratic Jews who had a visceral hatred for him no matter what he did. The Jewish Democrats were at the top his "Enemies List" because they would never agree with him on any issue. Even if he had been running against Heinrich Himmler, they would not have voted for him. The Israelis, however - the Jews living in Israel - were a very different story. To Nixon they were heroes, because he saw them as pioneers at the edge of the wilderness, standing up and fighting for what they believed in.

When did Nixon become aware of Israel's importance in world affairs? For an American politician, Nixon had a broad view of world affairs, heavily influenced by the Joe McCarthy years of Red-raving and baiting. He escaped the McCarthy crosshairs which often settled on his presidential boss, Dwight Eisenhower. Nixon envisioned breaking up the possible Communist alignment of the Soviets and the Red Chinese by opening relations and doing the unthinkable: going to China.

Because militarily the United States was still heavily entangled in Vietnam, little attention was paid to the Middle East.

The much larger problems of managing relations with and between China and the Soviet Union dominated Nixon's world view.

When suddenly attacked by Syria in 1970, Jordan's King Hussein sent a secret message to President Richard Nixon and Britain, pleading for defense of the Hashemite throne. Nixon, however, couldn't afford to flex his military muscles to shut down the intra-Arab war. When neither the U.S. nor Britain were able to help Jordan, Hussein's "Black September" problem was solved by their arch-enemy and next-door neighbor - Israel. The mobilized Israeli army moved against Syria's military western flank which had penetrated Jordan and were helping the Palestinians in their attempt to overthrow the Jordanian throne.

The Israeli threat caused the Syrian army to retreat northward into Syria. Without having to engage in combat, the very threat of an Israeli attack protected Jordan, the US Ally, and prevented the Soviets from encroaching further into the Middle East in support of its client states.

It was then that Nixon seemed to recognize the worldwide influence that little Israel could exert. He saw the tremendous potential of closer ties with Israel and of strengthening a junior partner in the on-going struggle of keeping Communism at bay. Israel took on a new luster in the president's vision of countering the Soviets and their allies.

While greatly admiring the Israelis and despising the Jewish Democrats, it never occurred to Nixon that both groups were Jewish. Understanding this aspect of his personality will shed light on why his actions and his language often seemed contradictory.

In June of 1967, the Israelis won stunning victories in the Six-Day War and decimated the Arab armies that came against them. Between the years of 1967 and 1973, many in the Israeli government and military developed an arrogant attitude toward the easily beaten enemy armies: "Ach, those Arabs! We can beat them easily. *No problemo."*
This dangerous attitude settled into the psyche of the Israeli people.

In October 1973, even though there had been intermittent shelling and some fighting between Israel and Egypt, no one believed an existential war over Israel was imminent. The Egyptian army had amassed on Israel's southern border, a tactic used on a regular basis, but this time Israel did not read it as a viable threat. For Israel, it was impossible to fall for every Egyptian feint and take each threat seriously by mobilizing their army. That meant calling up the army reservists who all had civilian jobs or ran businesses, again and again. It would wreak economic havoc and place a heavy emotional burden on their families as well.
Even today, the bulk of Israeli soldiers on active duty are the 18, 19 and 20-year old's that are just out of high school. The rest of the army is made up of reservists belonging to units that may train together a few times a year.

However, in the years following the Six Days War, because of their overwhelming victory many units were not even called up to train once a year. Prior to the Yom Kippur War, each time it appeared that Egypt was going to attack, Israel had to activate their reserves. Time and again the Egyptians did not follow through with an attack, so the Israeli reservists had to be deactivated to return to their civilian lives. With each military call-up, the fragile socialist-style economy suffered a severe jolt. Egypt's clever cat and mouse game lulled Israel into a hypnotic stupor.

On the eve of the 1973 war, the recurring Egyptian scenario looked exactly like so many previous ruses which raised the dilemma: "Can we afford to call up the army and shut down our economy - again?"
Both the Egyptians in the south and Syrians in the north were well coordinated in their plans, and their operational security was outstanding.

The **High Holy Days** (Hebrew: *Yamim Noraim*) "Days of Awe" are *Rosh Hashanah* ("Jewish New Year") and *Yom Kippur* ("Day of Atonement").
During the Ten Days of Repentance people contemplate on the personal, reflective, introspective aspects of their lives during the past year. It is customary to increase the giving of charity (*Tzedakah*) and to ask forgiveness from people one may have wronged. While judgment on each person is pronounced on *Rosh Hashanah*, it is not made absolute until *Yom Kippur*. The Ten Days are therefore an opportunity to mend one's ways in order to alter the judgment in one's favor. *Yom Kippur*, the Day of Atonement, is the holiest day of the year in Judaism. Its central themes are atonement and repentance. Jews traditionally observe this holy day with an approximate 25-hour period of fasting and intensive prayer, often spending most of the day in synagogue service s.

For the Jewish people, *Yom Kippur* 1973 was considered a double holy day because it fell on a Shabbat. That year, the Day of Atonement also coincided with the tenth day of Ramadan. Not only did Muslims celebrate Mohammed's first victory in his Jihad, holy war, but also commemorated the battle of Badr. In the year 624 BCE, the citizens of Mecca had been forced to become Muslims or die.

Yom Kippur Fast begins this evening

Jerusalem Post Staff

Tomorrow is Yom Kippur — the Day of Atonement. From sunset tonight until nightfall tomorrow, most Jews will be fasting and scheduled to return to Lod Airport today, and will be grounded there. The airport administration has warned all airlines that planes arriving this afternoon will not be

On the eve of the Yom Kippur War, this newspaper article talked about the fact that the whole country would come to a standstill. The army usually sent soldiers that were not needed home for this holiest day of the year. Even the non-religious Jews did not work. There was no public transportation or theater entertainment. Restaurants and shops were all closed; there were no radio or TV broadcasts. Most Israelis would spend the day either at home or in the synagogue. On Yom Kippur, even the most secular Israelis fast – they don't eat or drink (unless exempted for medical reasons) for 25 hours. By launching the attack on Yom Kippur, the Egyptians and Syrians caught Israel off guard. That Saturday, October 6, 1973, the Egyptian and Syrian armies, with advanced Soviet weapons, launched a two-front offensive on Israel.

AIR RAID SIRENS SHATTER STILLNESS OF YOM KIPPUR

At 2 p.m., air raid sirens shattered the peace and quiet of the most holy Jewish day. All military units frantically tried to contact their members, whether reservists or those on leave.

October 6 was a terrible wakeup call that had been perfectly planned by Israel's enemies. On the Israeli side of the Suez Canal, the Bar-Lev Line consisted of giant sand dunes where the IDF soldiers could safely operate and move behind, unseen by the enemy across the canal.

The Egyptians began their simultaneous air and artillery attacks by flying 250 Egyptian planes, MiG-21s, MiG-19s, and MiG-17s, attacking their assigned Israeli targets across the canal. Meanwhile, 2000 artillery pieces opened fire against all the strong points along the Israeli Line.

The barrage lasted 53 minutes. 10,500 shells fell in the first minute alone, or 175 shells per second.

For a long time, the Egyptians had been trying to find a way to get past, over or under those sand dunes without getting bogged down in a sand mountain.

Under cover of that massive air and artillery barrage, small boats with high pressure pumps and water cannons began blasting those sand dunes with water pumped from the canal. The giant sand piles rapidly disintegrated, allowing the Egyptian commandos to enter the breaches in what Israel thought was an impregnable embankment. Thirty-two thousand Egyptian soldiers attacked the 435 Israeli defenders along the entire canal.

The roads created by Egyptian engineers were shielded on each side by the remaining dunes.

While artillery was hitting the Israeli positions, Egyptian engineers assembled floating bridges at more than eighty breach points on the banks of the Egyptian side of the Suez Canal. These bridges supported Egyptian armor and tanks that had been cleverly camouflaged and staged close to the canal's edge. The Egyptian commandos killed most of the young (18 and 19- year old) IDF soldiers in their bunkers as they attempted to defend the line.

The whole Sinai was now open for Egyptian tanks to roll north to Beersheba, Ashdod, Ashkelon and the heartland of Israel. However, after crossing the canal and achieving complete surprise and having unstoppable momentum, in what appeared to be one of the great blunders of modern warfare, the Egyptian army stopped! The soldiers began digging in and waited for an Israeli counterattack. With hundreds of miles between the Egyptian and Israeli forces, this gave the IDF time to call up the reserves and move them to the front.
What happened next became a monumental disaster for the attackers.

Why did the Egyptians dig in and not Continue Through the Sinai After Gaining Such a Surprise Opening?

Only **Sadat** knew that he never intended to fight a full-fledged war against Israel. He secretly planned a surprise attack with an overwhelming force against the lightly held Israeli side of the canal. And then, after the initial victory, he had planned to STOP and hold in-place, because he wanted to break the impasse that had 'frozen'  the Mideast peace since 1967. In September of 1967, the leading Arab countries - Egypt, Iraq, Syria, Jordan, Lebanon, Kuwait, Algeria and Sudan - met in Khartoum, Sudan and adamantly declared their infamous three NO's after their disgraceful and shameful defeat by the Israelis.

125

The "Three No's" were: "No Peace with Israel, No Recognition of Israel and No Negotiations with Israel!" Sadat gambled that, if he could achieve a minor victory over the Israelis and then have the United Nations call for a cease fire, he would have regained enough honor in Egypt and perhaps in the Arab world that a political breakthrough could be achieved. In order to make it appear that this attack was really a part of a war that could bring the US and the Soviet Union into the beginning of WW III, Sadat also had to fool Syria and Jordan into joining the attack. But they never learned about his secret plan that his crossing the Suez Canal was as far as he intended to go. In effect, he double-crossed his fellow Arab leaders. Had they known about his limited intent, they never would have joined in. Of course, the Israeli leadership - headed by Prime Minister Golda Meir and Defense Minister Moshe Dayan - were also confused by Sadat's tactics.

Israel had a spy high up in the Egyptian command. **Ashraf Marwan,** son-in-law of late president Nasser, had morphed into a close advisor to President Sadat. Volunteering to spy for Israel soon after the Six-Day war, Marwan's Mossad code name was "Angel." Over the years, he had supplied Israel with extremely valuable information, but when planned Egyptian attacks were changed or cancelled, Israeli Intelligence began to discount his information. By the time of the Yom Kippur attack, "Angel's" information was only about four hours off as to when the war was to begin. However, Israel's command disregarded his warnings and failed to mobilize. This arrogant dismissal of purloined evidence eventually caused the most combat losses in the State's modern history.

Prior to the war, Golda Meir personally handed some of Marwan's reporting to President Nixon and Secretary of State Henry Kissinger. She informed them that Marwan had obtained copies of the minutes of a meeting between Sadat and Soviet leader Leonard Brezhnev.

Golda's reports passed to the president and the act of sharing classified, secret information deeply impressed both Nixon and Kissinger. In return, the president was willing to sell additional F-4 Phantoms to Israel. American Intelligence experts agreed with their Israeli counterparts that there would not be a war in 1973 because they all knew that Egypt couldn't win.

A short synopsis of one of their Top-Secret analyses read,
"Sadat's new campaign of threats to renew hostilities . . . are consistent both with preparations to fight Israel and with political/ psychological efforts to stimulate diplomatic activity . . . If Sadat is once again disappointed, the temptation to resort to military action in order to force the US hand might prove irresistible... Sadat himself could be trapped by building an atmosphere of crisis to the point where failure to act militarily would seem to him more dangerous to his own hold on power than attacking and taking the consequences."

In summary, in October 1973, the US analysts could not shake the compelling logic of Egypt's only fighting a winnable war, which it was in no position to launch. They overlooked the fact that Sadat also knew Egypt couldn't win, but he was willing to lose if he could attain a limited surprise victory before conceding to a cease fire with a limited gain. He knew that with his control of the news and propaganda on the Arab street, even a major defeat with a minor opening victory could elevate him to the pinnacle of the Arab pantheon.

Outmanned and outnumbered by soldiers and war material – it looked like defeat for Israel.

OPPOSING FORCES ON
THE EVE OF THE WAR

ISRAEL		ENEMY
358		998
FIGHTER JETS		FIGHTER JETS
2100		4350
TANKS		TANKS
37		137
NAVAL VESSELS		NAVAL VESSELS

THE WATERGATE SCANDAL

The Watergate scandal was a major federal political scandal involving the administration of President Richard Nixon from 1972 to 1974 that resulted in the end of Nixon's presidency. The scandal stemmed from the June 17, 1972, break-in of the Democratic National Committee (DNC) headquarters at the Watergate Office Building in Washington, D.C., by five men and the Nixon administration's subsequent attempts to cover up its involvement in the crime. Soon after the perpetrators were arrested, the press and the Justice Department discovered a connection between cash found on them at the time and a slush fund used by the Nixon re-election campaign committee. With his complicity in the cover-up made public and his political support completely eroded, Nixon resigned from office on August 9, 1974. To date, he is the only American president to have resigned from office. On September 8, 1974, Nixon's successor, Gerald Ford, pardoned him.

The term Watergate came to encompass an array of clandestine and often illegal activities undertaken by members of the Nixon administration. Those activities included bugging the offices of political opponents and people of whom Nixon or his officials were suspicious; ordering investigations of activist groups and political figures; and using the Federal Bureau of Investigation (FBI), the Central Intelligence Agency (CIA), and the Internal Revenue Service (IRS) as political weapons. The use of the suffix "-gate" after an identifying term (e.g. Bridgegate) has since become synonymous with public scandal, especially political scandal, in the United States and some other parts of the world.

Storm Clouds Over the White House.

Because of Watergate, both houses in Democratic hands and a Special Prosecutor dogging his every move, Nixon's life was falling apart. With the outbreak of the Yom Kippur War and the possibility of war with the Soviets, he received another blow.

His vice president Spiro Agnew resigned his office and was indicted amid revelations of corruption while governor and he did not contest his conviction.

In a letter to Fahd bin Abdul-Aziz Al Saud, then crown prince of Saudi Arabia, Agnew pleaded, *"I desperately need your financial support. Your Highness is already familiar with the unrelenting Zionist efforts to destroy me."* He added that the Zionists "framed" him. The reason, he also wrote, *"was that the Zionists in the United States knew that I would never agree to the continuance of the unfair and disastrous favoring of Israel, and they had to get me out of office there so that I would not succeed Nixon."*

VP Spiro Agnew and President Nixon

Agnew was known for his elaborate and articulate vocabulary, but this fawning letter revealed his true feelings about the "Zionists." He didn't use "Jews" but "Zionists", a relatively new term putting a political and regional spin on his perceived tormentors. Agnew's reasoning also reflected the same anti-Semitic rants of Nixon's closest aides Bob Haldeman and John Ehrlichman, revealed by the many Oval Office taped conversations.

Another dark cloud hovered over the president's head. Within two weeks, Nixon would be rebuffed by his own Attorney Generals when they resigned rather than fire the Special Prosecutor on Nixon's trail in the infamous "Saturday Night Massacre" of 20 October 1973.

The **Saturday Night Massacre** refers to the series of events that took place in the United States on the evening of Saturday, October 20, 1973, during the Watergate scandal. US President Richard Nixon ordered Attorney General Elliot Richardson to fire Special Prosecutor Archibald Cox; Richardson refused and resigned effective immediately. Nixon then ordered Deputy Attorney General William Ruckelshaus to fire Cox; Ruckelshaus refused, and also resigned. Nixon then ordered the third-most-senior official at the Justice Department, Solicitor General Robert Bork, to fire Cox. Bork considered resigning, but instead carried out the dismissal as Nixon asked. The political and public reactions to Nixon's actions were negative and highly damaging to the president. The impeachment process against Richard Nixon began 10 days later, on October 30, 1973. New Special Prosecutor Leon Jaworski was appointed on November 1, 1973, and on November 14, 1973, United States District Judge Gerhard Gesell ruled that the dismissal had been illegal.

The Situation in Israel

During this time, relations between Israel and the USA were all right but not overly close.

On the 9th of October, Golda Meir called the Israeli Ambassador to the United States (Simcha Dinitz) and demanded that he call Henry Kissinger right away.

Moshe Dayan, Golda Meir, Simcha Dinitz and Henry Kissinger

However, at 1:45 a.m. Washington time, Kissinger was asleep.

Golda told Dinitz to vividly convey the seriousness of Israel's situation. Also, using his best diplomatic language, he was to let Secretary Kissinger know that Israel's precarious position was mostly because he (Kissinger) had previously let her know that any preemptive strike on Israel's part would be met with heavy disapproval from the US and no assistance if they were to ask for it.

Golda reminded Dinitz that she had made the wrenching decision not to strike the Arabs in any preemptive attack, as they did in 1967. She emphasized that the Israeli Government understood that if they attacked first, even to defend themselves, no one would help them, not even the United States.

Henry Kissinger said later, *"If Israel attacked first, the United States would not have supplied Israel with so much as a nail."*

Israel absorbed the first blows. Because that option of preemption (so successfully used in the Six-Day War) was not available, Israel was now in a life and death situation and needed immediate triage.

Golda also emphatically insisted that Ambassador Dinitz was to clearly hint that Israel might be pushed to consider using its 'Doomsday' device . That was an unspoken threat to use the nuclear option if help couldn't be obtained very soon.

"It's no accident many accuse me of conducting public affairs with my heart instead of my head. Well, what if I do? Those who don't know how to weep with their whole heart don't know how to laugh either." Golda Meir

Kissinger quietly listened, understood and hastily arranged an early morning meeting in his office. Thoroughly briefed on Israel's heavy losses, Kissinger certainly was informed of Israel's decision "to defer but not rule out" the possibility of utilizing their nuclear weapon. Neither Kissinger nor Meir would acknowledge that such a message even existed, because both sides had long ago decided that it was an issue better kept under wraps. Later, when briefing the president, it is reported that Kissinger referred to Nixon's 1969 meeting with PM Meir when he said, *"During your private discussions with Golda Meir, you emphasized that our primary concern was that Israel make no visible introduction of nuclear weapons or undertake a nuclear test program."* Nixon acknowledged that secret and yet informal agreement.

That 1969 meeting between Nixon and Meir set what has been Israel's unofficial policy ever since: one in which the country does nothing to publicly acknowledge or demonstrate its nuclear weapons program, and in exchange the United States would quietly accept it and would not pressure Israel into signing a nuclear non-proliferation treaty (which would have caused Israel to acknowledge that they do have a nuclear weapon capacity).

Israel has never publicly acknowledged that capacity, but every country in the world is convinced they have that secret weapon.

Nixon's Background

Nixon's parents were Quakers and through her religious background, his mother certainly understood the importance of the Jews.

"One day, Richard," she told him when he was still a young boy, "you will be in a powerful position and a situation will arise where Israel and the Jews will need your help. When it does, you are to help them!"

Nixon (second from right) makes his newspaper debut in 1916, contributing five cents to a fund for war orphans.

Richard Nixon often told of that long-ago incident. Isn't it exciting and revealing to find the time and place when such an important seed was planted in a young child's life?

During that long-ago moment in that tiny house his father built near the family's lemon orchard in Yorba Linda, California, it undoubtedly made little sense to young Richard.

Even when someone says something to you and you file it in the back of your mind, that tiny seed is still there. And then, for some reason, there comes a time when it sprouts and starts to grow.

In Nixon's case, Golda's request for help echoed his mother's voice and her prediction.

Stories have circulated that Golda called Nixon at 3 a.m., pleading for help, and he remembered his mother's voice telling him about helping the Jews. It's a good story, but is there any verification of that incident? What if the 3 a.m. phone call from Golda to Richard Nixon never happened? Other than a few Christian blogs, which seem to repeat the story verbatim, this writer was unable to find any source that documented the call in either Israeli or US documents.

But, even if there wasn't a personal phone call, the plea got through. The Israeli PM called her ambassador in DC, who called the Secretary of State, who eventually relayed the message to the president.

The president recognized the threat that an Arab victory would in effect be the "victory of and by Soviet arms." Being the Arab world's chief supplier of munitions, the Soviets were strategically attempting to spread its influence throughout the region. Nixon rightly feared that other Arab countries would flock to the Soviet armaments, which would open the gates to further Soviet influence in the region. Nixon was always thinking of how he could blunt further Communist influence from spreading. Of course, this view was all part and parcel of the "Cold War", when Communism was at its apex.

Nixon knew that the only way to end the crisis and push out the Communist influence was to provide American arms to the Israelis in order to defeat the Soviet arms in the hands of the Syrians and Egyptians. Knowing that the Soviets were rapidly resupplying Egypt and Syrian losses and their transit route was much shorter, it was imperative that the resupply was launched as quickly as possible.

Realizing the world-wide ramifications of the conflict, Nixon told Kissinger that Israel truly needed America's help. He ordered him to send everything they asked for. "I'm not letting Israel go down!" he emphatically exclaimed.

Deliveries of supplies, including aircraft, had to be sped up and Israel be told that it could freely expend all of its consumables — ammunition, spare parts, fuel, and so forth — in the certain knowledge that these would be completely replenished by the United States without any delay.

White House Chief of Staff **Alexander Haig** concurred.

As soon as the scope and pattern of Israeli battle losses emerged, Nixon ordered, *"that all destroyed equipment be made up out of U.S. stockpiles, using the very best weapons America possesses. Whatever it takes - save Israel!"*

Nixon, however, forgot about the slow wheels of bureaucracy and the infighting that occurred within his own administration. The president may give the word on Pennsylvania Avenue, but

Alexander Haig

politics and personalities are involved before it can be implemented. Some may have stood up and said, "Yes sir! Yes sir! - three bags full," and immediately began their small part of a large task that had never been done before. Others however, 'sandbagged' the orders by doing their jobs in slow motion.

Sand was also thrown into the proverbial gear box by the internal jealousies and gamesmanship between two Jews in the administration.

It was clear that Kissinger and **James Schlesinger,** the Secretary of Defense were no friends.

Born to a Jewish mother from Lithuania, Schlesinger later rejected his Jewish background and heritage by converting to Lutheranism.

Some writers have argued that all his life he remained deeply conflicted about his ethnic identity. This may account for the conflict he experienced with Kissinger as he opposed him at every

Schlesinger

opportunity. Schlesinger apparently shared the anti-Israel position of his Deputy Secretary of Defense, **William Clements**, an oilman with pro-Arab sympathies. Together they precipitated a four-day delay in starting a weapons airlift to resupply Israel after its initial war losses became known to the administration.

Clements

When Kissinger told Schlesinger to begin sending all that material to Israel, Schlesinger kept coming up with excuses for the delays so that when Nixon asked if the ammunition and weapons were sent, Kissinger told him about the hold ups.

On the audio tapes, you can hear the president using a lot of expletives as he hears the bad news. *"You get your ### out of here and tell those people to move!"*

Frustrated by the delays in implementing the airlift and aware that the Soviets had begun their own shipments of supplies to Egypt and Syria, Nixon summoned Kissinger and Schlesinger to the Oval Office on October 12 and "banished all excuses." He demanded a list of everything that Israel needed, which Kissinger read aloud. "Just double everything on that list and get your (expletives) out of the office and see that the job is done!" Nixon ordered.

When Kissinger told the president that the Air Force didn't want to fly certain planes, Nixon became incensed.
"Use every plane we have and send everything that can fly!" he shouted.

Schlesinger initially wanted to send just three transports to Israel because he feared anything more would alarm the Arabs and the Soviets. Nixon snapped: *"We are going to get blamed just as much for three as for 300. . . . Get them in the (expletive) air, now!"*
But then it was Europe's turn to balk and block. "Now wait a minute! We can't have you overflying Europe! If we do that, the Arabs are going to hate us, and we need their oil."

The US Air Force found a way to bypass Europe and fly via the Mediterranean. They received permission to refuel on the Canary Islands with the help of Portugal and the Netherlands.

On the 14th of October, five days after the start of the fighting, and after what must have seemed an eternity to Israeli commanders, the US Air Force started delivering the vitally needed supplies.

The actual speed of delivery was due in part to the intervention by someone with a long history of admiring Israel. Nixon's Chief of Staff, Alexander Haig, played a unique role in this endeavor. The moment Haig, a retired Army general, realized what was going on, he acted. Bypassing the Defense and State Departments, he began calling US military bases and building stockpiles of items the Israelis needed.

Even though he was no longer in the chain of command or authorized to do this, the troops listened to him. He was able to get it out of the warehouses and ready to go, including some of our newest weapons which were still embargoed.

Always motivated by his broad international world view, President Nixon immediately saw an opportunity where he could stop the growing influence of the Soviet Union. He didn't just see weapons. He saw SOVIET weapons, SOVIET advisors and SOVIET tactics.

If they could be defeated by American weaponry in the hands of the Israelis, it would be a massive SOVIET defeat. Helping Israel defeat the Soviet proxies fit neatly into his worldview and so, US combat cargo was readied. El Al Israeli airplanes had their national identities painted over and were launched. Nixon was extremely anxious to get the resupply airlift off the ground.

This action on the world stage was also a distraction from the constant drumbeat of an impending impeachment. At that time, he was knee-deep in the Watergate swamp and each day sucked further down. He needed to be back on that world stage in a positive role, like his breakthrough visit to China in 1972. Perhaps he envisioned that he might emerge from this Arab-Israeli war as a peacemaker worthy of world acclaim, which would dampen the Watergate accusations that continued to dog him. Maybe he even glimpsed a Nobel Peace Prize in the offing.

Operation Nickel Grass was a strategic airlift operation conducted by the United States to deliver weapons and supplies to Israel during the 1973 Yom Kippur War. In a series of events that took place over 32 days, the U.S. Air Force's Military Airlift Command shipped 22,325 tons of tanks, artillery, ammunition, and supplies in C-141 Starlifter and C-5 Galaxy transport aircraft between 14 October and 14 November 1973. The U.S. support helped ensure that Israel survived a coordinated and surprise attack from the Soviet-backed Arab Republic of Egypt and Syrian Arab Republic. Following a U.S. pledge of support on 19 October, the oil-exporting Arab states within the Organization of Petroleum Exporting Countries (OPEC) held to their previously declared warnings to use oil as a "weapon" and declared a complete oil embargo on the United States, and restrictions on other countries. This, along with the contemporaneous failure of major pricing and production negotiations between the exporters and the major oil companies, led to the 1973 oil crisis.

When Schlesinger finally followed the president's orders, thanks to Alexander Haig's foresightedness and initiative, the majority of the material was magically and logistically ready to load and be airlifted to Israel.

Code-named "**Operation Nickel Grass**", 567 flying missions delivered over 22,000 tons of supplies to Israel. An additional 90,000 tons were delivered by sea. By the beginning of December, Israel had received nearly 40 F-4 fighter-bombers, 46 A-4 attack airplanes, 12 C-130 cargo airplanes, 8 CH-53 helicopters, 40 unmanned aerial vehicles, 200 M-60/ M-48A3 tanks, 250 armored personnel carriers, 226 utility vehicles, 12 MIM-72 Chaparral surface-to-air missile systems, three MIM-23 Hawk surface-to-air missile systems, 36 155 mm artillery pieces, seven 175 mm artillery pieces, and large quantities of 105 mm, 155 mm and 175 mm ammunition. State of the art equipment, such as the AGM-65 Maverick missile and the BGM-71 TOW - weapons that had only entered production a few years prior - as well as highly advanced electronic jamming equipment were also sent.

Most of the combat airplanes arrived during the war, and most were taken directly from United States Air Force units. Most of the larger equipment arrived after the ceasefire.

"Israel is the largest American aircraft carrier in the world that cannot be sunk. It does not carry even one American soldier, and it's located in a critical region for American national security."

Alexander Haig

Of all the people, Haig understood and was a true friend of Israel, not only during the Nixon administration but years later in the Reagan administration. But that's another story.

"The airlift that the USA brought, all this equipment to us, we were astounded by it. At that point, we didn't even ask for an airlift. This was beyond our imagination."
The voice of Prime Minister Meir's aide quivered with grateful appreciation.

OPERATION
NICKEL
GRASS
Airlift in Support of
National Policy

The arrival of the American planes turned the course of the Yom Kippur War.

In the weeks that followed the Yom Kippur war, Nixon and Golda Meir became very close.

At the end of her life, Golda said: "President Nixon was MY president." Golda's sister lived in the USA and like so many Democratic Jews, she hated Nixon. Golda wrote to her sister: *"Nixon is the best president there ever was. He saved Israel and you better understand that."*

After the war, Golda went to the USA to personally thank Nixon.

"As President Nixon says, presidents can do almost anything, and President Nixon has done many things that nobody would have thought of doing."   Golda Meir

Because of the Watergate scandal, this was one of the last laughs that Nixon had publicly. Soon thereafter, he was to be the only American president ever to resign the high office.

Shortly after the Yom Kippur war, the Israeli PM told a group of Jewish leaders in Washington, *"For generations to come, all will be told of the miracle of the immense planes from the United States bringing in the material that meant life to our people."*

Shortly before his resignation Nixon flew to Israel, where he received a heroic welcome.

Israelis will never forget the airlift which was forcefully directed by Richard M. Nixon, whom many Jews believed to be the world's foremost anti-Semite.

During one of my trips to Israel, I had the privilege of taking one of those pilots with me. The moment Israelis found out (he didn't say anything, but I told them) that he had been a pilot in that Yom Kippur airlift, he was treated with the greatest respect wherever we went.

We owe that to Richard Nixon, whom God put in that seat, right there in the White House.

As Israeli Ambassador Ron Dermer said,
"When someone does something exceptionally good (or exceptionally bad) for the Jewish people, it becomes part of our living history, and they become immortalized forever for their actions."

Ron Dermer

No matter what the world thinks about Nixon, even though he knew that his world was crashing down, he had the courage and strength to do what was right - no matter the consequences.

His actions during the 1973 Yom Kippur War were undoubtedly the reason that God had elevated him to that position In Israel's greatest time of need. The man was already in place to carry out the will of the Lord in strengthening Israel so they could overcome those who were bent on their destruction. Nixon did what was right.

It was Nixon who made Israel the largest recipient of US foreign aid; he also initiated the policy of virtually limitless U.S. weapons sales to Israel. The notion of Israel as a strategic asset to the United States, not just a moral commitment, was also Nixon's innovation.

Nixon ordered the greatest American resupply effort to an ally at war, and in desperate need, in history. The resupply effort had to be done mostly by airlift, because time was of the essence. Compounding the difficulty of resupply, practically every European country, NATO ally or not, denied the United States permission to land, refuel or load on their way to help Israel. They even denied American planes over-flight permission. The Europeans were terrified of the Arab Oil Embargo Weapon. Nixon's persistent driving of Kissinger and Schlesinger made the resupply possible in record time and amount.

Richard Milhous Nixon increased our military and financial support to Israel and was there in their time of existential need. By blessing them, our nation was also blessed by his decisions and actions. Thank God!

Nixon became the first sitting president to visit Israel - the only democratic friend the United States has in the Middle East. Sensing that his days in the government were limited, he wanted to spend it with friends who appreciated what he had done for them.

Golda Meir, Chaim Herzog, Yitzhak Rabin

Golda Meir, described as the toughest 'man' in Ben Gurion's cabinet, admitted that upon hearing of the airlift during a cabinet meeting, she began to cry uncontrollably.

Chaim Herzog, Israel's sixth president, said, *"He (Nixon) supplied arms and unflinching support when our very existence would have been in danger without them."*

Yitzhak Rabin, a former IDF Chief of Staff, Ambassador to the US and Israeli Prime Minister, said in an Israeli radio interview that no president in American history had been more committed to Israel's security than Richard Nixon.

In 1976, three years after the event, The New York Times reported that Kissinger delayed the airlift because he wanted to see Israel *"bleed just enough to soften it up for the post-war diplomacy he was planning."*

Other sources stated, *"Kissinger had urged Nixon to delay the airlift so as to let Israel 'bleed a little', in the hopes that a badly bruised Israel would be more pliable to concessions in post-war negotiations, but Nixon refused."* Thank God!

A "little bloodied"? "Bleed a little"?

In retrospect the war resulted in 2,688 dead and hundreds of badly wounded Israeli soldiers.

When Kissinger's remarks are paired with the casualty figures, it paints a sordid picture of an intellectual who could put his view of manipulating world leaders and events above the lives of soldiers. The Secretary of State also feared that another overwhelming Israeli victory *"would cause Israel to strengthen its resolve not to make any territorial concessions in Sinai."*
Of course, these statements were denied by Kissinger, but his analytical cold-hearted demeanor remains even today, and it is thought that he likely did say it.

Of course, statements like that were a shock to the Jewish world, who expected a German-Jewish American to be much more pro-Israel in his advice to the president. *If* he said it (and that's a big if), he may have said it to more closely ingratiate himself with the power troika of Nixon, Haldeman and Erlichman, whom Kissinger knew were very anti-Semitic in all their conversations and plotting. Perhaps he was attempting to protect his job (he was always overly protective and sensitive) by becoming "one of the boys" and not the token "court Jew."

At the time of the Yom Kippur War, he was both National Security Advisor (NSA) and the Secretary of State. It was also a time when Nixon was suspected of drinking heavily and being increasingly erratic. Kissinger may have wanted to impress his boss with how "hard" and "tough minded" he could be, which obviously would have impressed anyone who always talked that way behind closed doors. On the other hand, it may very well have been his real personality and world view that was being exposed.

The Israeli leaders never saw Kissinger as a friend to be counted on because he was Jewish.
During an impasse in one of his shuttle diplomacy trips to Israel, Kissinger was being extremely harsh. Prime Minister Golda Meir reprimanded her fellow Jew by asking him why he was being so hard on Israel.

Kissinger responded in his low and slow, heavily accented German response, *"Madame Prime Minister, it is imperative that you remember that first and foremost I am an American, second that I am the Secretary of State and the National Security Advisor to the president of the United States, and thirdly I happen to be a Jew."*
Golda responded, *"Cousin Henry, you forget that here in Israel we Jews read from right to left."*

What did Nixon set in motion with his resupply that eventually changed the relationship between Israel and the United States?

Following the Yom Kippur War, Israel began to receive about $2.1 billion a year, half in loans and half in grants. Almost all the money had to be used to purchase American-made military hardware. Five years later, Israel began to receive $3 billion in grants as a result of the Camp David Accords, which led to the 1979 Israeli-Egyptian peace treaty.

With Israel feeling more secure, the United States embarked on an ambitious Middle East peace process. Disengagement agreements after the war led to direct peace talks.

Begin - Carter - Sadat

Six years later these culminated in the Camp David Accords between Israel and Egypt.

The Camp David Accords were signed by Egyptian President Anwar Sadat and Israeli Prime Minister Menachem Begin on 17 September 1978, following twelve days of secret negotiations at Camp David. The two framework agreements were signed at the White House, and were witnessed by President Jimmy Carter. The second of these frameworks (A Framework for the Conclusion of a Peace Treaty between Egypt and Israel) led directly to the 1979 Egypt–Israel Peace Treaty. Due to the agreement, Sadat and Begin received the shared 1978 Nobel Peace Prize. The first framework (A Framework for Peace in the Middle East), which dealt with the Palestinian territories, was written without participation of the Palestinians and was condemned by the United Nations.

Israeli recognition in that treaty of the Palestinian cause eventually spurred the Oslo Accords between Israel and the Palestinians. They were the basis of a long-running peace process which ultimately failed. However, none of the agreements would have been possible without Israel's victory in the Yom Kippur War. As a direct result of the war, the United States quadrupled its foreign aid to Israel, replacing France as Israel's largest arms supplier. In fact, the doctrine of maintaining Israel's "qualitative edge" over its neighbors was born in the war's aftermath.

Fifteen years after leaving the presidency, Richard Nixon was still thinking globally and giving advice to presidents and other world leaders.

In an August 8, 1989 memo (unsolicited?) to President George H. W. Bush, President Nixon urged his successor and one-time protege to use his electoral mandate to set a new direction of policy for the long-term interests of America and its allies in the Middle East.

Then Congressman G.W. Bush and President Nixon

Though Nixon believed that the United States should maintain close ties with its democratic ally, Israel, he argued that it would be disastrous not to do more to extend goodwill to nearby Arab states. The Israelis had won every war they fought since their independence in 1948.

However, each subsequent war had come at an increasing cost in blood and treasure. The Arabs were learning how to fight, and their exponential population growth gave them a favorable geopolitical advantage over the Israelis.

"Israel will inevitably become even more than now a tiny garrison island-state in a sea of implacable enemies."

Nixon recalled how French President Charles De Gaulle told him that the United States needed to recognize China while it was still weak, before its full potential was realized. Israel was in a similar position, and it could gain more diplomatic goodwill while it still had a strategic advantage over the Arabs.

Nixon then signaled to the ripening positive developments in the region. Palestinian leader Yasser Arafat's recognition of Israel's right to exist wouldn't have been a thought in years past. In Israel, the domestic political situation was more favorable than ever to negotiations with the Palestinians.

Furthermore, the Soviet's declining influence in the region also reduced any potential for a clash between the world's great powers. Nixon's prescription called for US leadership to confer America's prestige on the peacemaking process while defending Israel and opening dialogue to major actors in the Middle East.

Specifically, he counseled Bush to shape U.S. policy in the following manner:

— Help secure the border of Israel and encourage them to exchange land for peace.

— Allow for self-government of Palestinians, but not an armed Palestinian state.

— Push for Vatican oversight of Holy sites.

— Don't support an international conference: Israel would be alone and submit its fate to a stacked jury.

— Find a strong negotiator. Select a person outside the Foreign Service or National Security Council. Give the negotiator plenty of time, at least two years, to accomplish his or her goals.

— Authorize the negotiator to talk with Arafat. Peace might not be achieved with him. But it certainly won't be achieved without him.

— Consider a Mutual Defense Treaty with Israel. This would enlist Israel's support and allow for greater latitude in negotiations.

"As I complete this letter, I almost hesitate to sign it and send it to you," Nixon concluded, recalling the difficulty in dealing with this part of the world as vice president under Eisenhower during the 1956 Suez Crisis, and as president during the 1973 Yom Kippur War.

"In the interests of Israel as well as our own interests, you should insist that the only way to assert the survival of Israel is for the U.S. to support an initiative which has some chance to bring peace to the world's most explosive area." Dick

"The more you stay in this kind of job, the more you realize that a public figure, a major public figure, is a lonely man."

Nixon's parents and siblings

Nixon and his mother, Hannah

AMERICA NEEDS

NIXON!

THIS TIME

VOTE like your whole
world depended on it.

VOTE the entire REPUBLICAN slate!

Distributed by
CALIFORNIA CITIZENS FOR NIXON-AGNEW

NIXON QUOTES

♦ "Defeat doesn't finish a man, quit does. A man is not finished when he's defeated. He's finished when he quits."

♦ "You've got to learn to survive a defeat. That's when you develop character."

♦ "Never let your head hang down. Never give up and sit down and grieve. Find another way. And don't pray when it rains if you don't pray when the sun shines."

PART 4

RONALD REAGAN

Ronald Wilson Reagan - 1911- 2004

Ronald Reagan was an American politician who served as the 40th president of the United States from 1981 to 1989. Prior to his presidency, he was a Hollywood actor and union leader, President of the Screen Actors Guild, Governor of California and Chair of the Republican Governors Association. Reagan was preceded by Jimmy Carter and succeeded by George H.W. Bush.

INTRODUCTION

During his two times in office, Ronald Reagan, the 40th President of the United States, was never particularly regarded as a great friend or benefactor of Israel. During the eight-year Reagan-time-in-office of the 1980's a number of speed bumps jarred the American Jewish community on a regular basis.

Prior to Reagan running for governor in California or for the presidency of the United States, he had always been staunchly pro-Israel and pro-Jewish. At the end of World War II, when the Holocaust atrocities were revealed, he never forgot the horror he felt watching films of the Nazis' genocide of the Jews.

Reagan and 'Ike'

However, when Reagan first ran for governor of California in 1966, he was charged with being anti-Semitic. Former President Dwight David "Ike" Eisenhower gave Reagan some behind-the-scenes advice to help him fight those false charges. On June 11, 1967, the newly elected Governor Reagan spoke at a huge pro-Israel rally at the Hollywood Bowl. The event had been quickly organized after Israel's stunning and victorious Six-Day War. That war began on Monday morning, June 5, with a preemptive strike against 14 Egyptian airfields. It effectively destroyed Egypt's Air Force and assured the destruction of Egypt's armed forces who were now without air cover. One of its military triumphs was Israel recapturing Jerusalem. The Israeli government vowed that the city never again would be divided and be Israel's capital forever. In his speech addressing world affairs, candidate Reagan delivered a stinging rebuke to Lyndon Johnson's plan for the US to remain neutral.

Johnson's neutrality contrasted with Reagan's beliefs, which he forcefully stated in his Hollywood Bowl maiden foreign policy speech. "America must not remain neutral when it comes to Israel. America has the moral obligation to support the Middle East's only democracy!"

Johnson felt the USA was unable to aid Israel because of our heavy Vietnam involvement. From a recorded Oval Office phone call, we learn that he counseled Israeli Prime Minister Eshkol to "let the bad guys draw first and then you can shoot them!" It sounded as if he had just watched another episode of "Gunsmoke". In effect, Johnson told Israel to absorb the first blow so that, if the US stepped in, it would be seen as a neutral peacemaker. After finishing the call, Johnson remarked to an aide, "I know damn well that they [the Israelis] are going to hit them first." At that moment, Syrian, Egyptian and Jordanian armies had been mobilized on Israel's borders. All the Arab nations joined in the chorus of "Death to Israel! We'll attack and wipe Israel off the map!"

Even though Israel tried to live in peace, it was threatened and attacked in 1948, 1956, 1967 and again in October 1973.

With a distinct moral and biblical basis, Reagan stated loud and clear, "Our national interest is inextricably woven into the fabric of Israel."

In the following years, Reagan saw the decisions he and America had to make in light of moral and biblical terms of right versus wrong. Around the same time, in another speech Reagan mentioned where the aftermath of the Six Day War would likely be debated by America and the rest of the world. He knew that the United Nations would force a settlement upon Israel.

At the General Assembly, small nations had power and at the Security Council, the Soviet Union could veto a vote. Reagan stated that the United Nations, "as presently constituted," was exactly the wrong place to have final negotiations. According to him, the only parties directly involved, meaning only Israel and the attacking Arab armies which had waged the fighting, could negotiate with each other.

There are no easy answers, but there are simple answers. We must have the courage to do what we know is morally right.

RESOLUTION 242

Security Council
United Nations

United Nations Security Council Resolution 242 was adopted unanimously by the UN Security Council on November 22, 1967, in the aftermath of the Six Day War. It was adopted under Chapter VI of the United Nations Charter. The preamble refers to the "inadmissibility of the acquisition of territory by war and the need to work for a just and lasting peace in the Middle East in which every State in the area can live in security." Operative Paragraph One "Affirms that the fulfillment of Charter principles requires the establishment of a just and lasting peace in the Middle East which should include the application of both the following principles:

(i) Withdrawal of Israel armed forces from territories occupied in the recent conflict;

(ii) Termination of all claims or states of belligerency and respect for and acknowledgment of the sovereignty, territorial integrity and political independence of every State in the area and their right to live in peace within secure and recognized boundaries free from threats or acts of force."

Resolution 242 is one of the most commonly referenced UN resolutions to end the Arab–Israeli conflict, and the basis of later negotiations between the parties. Egypt, Jordan, Israel and Lebanon entered into consultations with the UN Special representative over the implementation of 242. After denouncing it in 1967, Syria "conditionally" accepted the resolution in March 1972. Syria formally accepted UN Security Council Resolution 338, the cease-fire at the end of the Yom Kippur War (in 1973), which embraced resolution 242.

This resolution continues to be the formula proposed by the Security Council for the successful resolution of the Arab-Israeli conflict, in particular, ending the state of belligerency then existing between the 'States concerned', Israel and Egypt, Jordan, Syria and Lebanon. The resolution deals with five principles; withdrawal of Israeli forces, 'peace within secure and recognized boundaries, freedom of navigation, a just settlement of the refugee problem and security measures including demilitarized zones'. It also provided for the appointment of a Special Representative to proceed to the Middle East in order to promote agreement on a peaceful and accepted settlement in accordance with the principles outlined in the resolution.

The result of that debate led to UN Resolution 242. More than a half century later it still is the governing international law that is in effect to this very day. There still is no resolution to the problem.

Reagan's share of the Jewish vote in the 1980 election was 39 percent – the best showing among Jews for a Republican presidential candidate since Dwight Eisenhower's 40 percent in 1956.

However, the number that really stands out after all these years is that while Reagan won a 44-state blowout victory in the nation at large, a fully 61 percent of Jewish voters preferred either the incumbent Jimmy Carter, or third-party candidate John Anderson.

Several presidential administrations have deliberately distanced themselves from Israel, believing that this would produce payoffs with the Arabs. Presidents Eisenhower, Nixon, Carter, Bush-41 and Obama believed that their predecessors had been too close to the Israelis and that closeness had negatively cost the United States dearly with the Arabs and Europeans. Following the Jimmy Carter and his National security Advisor Zbigniew Brzezinski years, regaining confidence and rebuilding the alliance with Israel should have been a relatively easy act for Reagan to follow.

A few Reagan Quotes

- Politics is supposed to be the second-oldest profession. I have come to realize that it bears a very close resemblance to the first.
- Within the covers of the Bible are the answers for all the problems men face.
- I have wondered at times what the Ten Commandments would have looked like if Moses had run them through the US Congress.

Reagan's Middle East Philosophy

Initially, Reagan's Middle East philosophy was summarized as follows: First, he believed in a militarily strong Israel, which he viewed as both democratic and anti-Soviet. He characterized the Jewish state in 1980 as "the only remaining strategic asset in the region on which we can rely." (Washington Post, August 1979).

Secondly, he believed in Israel's unremitting fight against terrorism and its resistance to Jimmy Carter's constant calls for moderation in retaliation. Reagan was also personally opposed to the Palestinian's incessant demands for their own state. He had been a serious long-time student of Communism and firmly believed that a Palestinian State would unquestionably be a surrogate of the Soviet Union.

Jews have had a long and at times complicated relationship with the men who have served as presidents of the United States. Leaders like Woodrow Wilson and Harry Truman cannot be summed up in a paragraph, especially when examining their thoughts and actions toward Jews. An examination of Ronald Reagan's relationship with the state of Israel and especially the Prime Ministers during his terms would best be described as mixed. Although some writers and boosters continue to describe Reagan as an unflagging friend of the state of Israel, those eight years were often very strained.

For all the Reagan-Begin disagreements, the US-Israel relationship came out stronger than it was when their respective terms in office began. It seems that Reagan had a special affinity for Jews, which stemmed from a multitude of factors – his personal ecumenical nature; his often told

reminiscences about his Catholic father's stubborn intolerance of religious, racial, and ethnic discrimination; and his Protestant mother's oft repeated instruction that her son "love thy neighbor." He certainly learned these virtues at a young age growing up in the heart of the midwestern "Land of Lincoln." As **Bill Clark**, a devout Catholic and one of Reagan's closest aides, put it: "He was very tolerant of other faiths, especially the Jewish faith."

Reagan and the Soviet Jews

What was it that impelled Reagan to single out the plight of the Soviet Jews in particular? Was there a seed planted early in his youth that sprouted and grew and came into full bloom 50 or 60 years later? Perhaps the earliest documented example of Reagan learning about the suffering of Russian Jews was when he heard a guest speaker at his church in Dixon, Illinois on November 11, 1928.

That evening, the First Christian Church on South Hennepin Avenue hosted a Russian Jew named B.E. Kertchman, whose speech offered a modern history of Jews and their relations with other peoples and nations.

Reagan's boyhood home

Kertchman was recruited by the enthusiastic church pastor, Ben Cleaver, who was like a second father to the young Ronald Reagan because his Catholic father was often AWOL. His mother, Nelle was very active in the local protestant churches and had a great influence on her boys' later lives.

Clearly, young "Dutch" Reagan was not ignorant of the plight of the Jewish people. Reagan's interest in Jewish issues intensified after leaving his home state of Illinois and his move to California.

His acting career opened a door into politics, especially through his position as president of the Screen Actors Guild (SAG).

Reagan's family - he is about 2 years old in this picture

"Freedom prospers when religion is vibrant and the rule of law under God is acknowledged."

Reagan, SAG and DP's

While historians have rightly connected Reagan's work at SAG with the start of his fight against Communism, they have somehow managed to miss his first public confrontation with the USSR in this period.

As president of SAG, Reagan spoke on behalf of the so-called "Displaced Persons" (Dps).

DPs initially were survivors of World War II Nazism, primarily Jews. Once the war ended, the list of DP-designated peoples widened to include 1.5 million individuals escaping Soviet-occupied areas in Eastern Europe, though they still included numerous Jews who longed for the creation of a homeland in Palestine.

1960 SAG membership meeting

The DPs were held in camps in Britain, Canada, Belgium, and Latin America, at a large cost to the United States – at least $100 million annually. Soviet officials outrageously claimed that the US was holding the DPs as a source of semi-slave labor – a charge dismissed by Eleanor Roosevelt as "utterly untrue."

A bill was introduced in Congress by William G. Stratton, a Republican congressman from Reagan's home state, to permit entry of 400,000 DPs into the States. Reagan fought for the bill, which faced stiff opposition in Congress. He did not shy from dramatic rhetoric, agreeing with UN official Herbert H. Lehman: "Apparently there are some people who would rather bury the Stratton bill in red tape and thus bury the DPs in a mass grave. They would be burying Protestants, Catholics, and Jews alike."

Lehman

On May 7, 1947, Reagan, through the New York-based Citizens Committee on Displaced Persons, released a statement urging passage of the Stratton bill. This was probably his first open campaign against Moscow, and it involved defending people of all faiths, including Jews.

158

Reagan and the Communists

Ronald Reagan first came to the attention of many conservatives by his unswerving interest in and ability to articulate the dangers of Communism. During the "Red Scare" days of the early fifties, Wisconsin Senator Joe McCarthy ranted about communism's danger to the West.

This theme was picked up by the clean-cut, boy-next-door type who was the exact opposite of the "heavy" drunken McCarthy.

As president of the Screen Actors Guild, Reagan faced an entrenched group of communist writers who had infiltrated the ranks of Hollywood's studios. In 1962, Ronald Reagan was the narrator of a documentary named, "The Truth About Communism."

He didn't just read a script but became immersed in studying the subject. The truth about communism always seemed to be at the forefront of his worldview.

"How do you tell a Communist? Well, it's someone who reads Marx and Lenin. And how do you tell an anti-Communist? It's someone who understands Marx and Lenin."   Reagan

One of the most instructive insights into Reagan's connection with Jews relates to his Cold War experience and study of the world-wide struggle between the West and the forces of Communism, which he interpreted as the most important battle of the post-war 20th century.

Nothing animated Reagan more than his goal of undermining atheistic Soviet Communism and thereby liberating millions of people enslaved under it. It was the Jews imprisoned behind the Iron Curtain who were a central part of that calling.

America's own Conservative Revolution

In 1980, three years after Israel elected its first conservative Likud government, the United States also ushered in a conservative revolution of its own, one that would have dramatic ramifications for American foreign policy. Under Ronald Reagan, America would no longer seek détente with the Soviet Union, as it did under Jimmy Carter, and the United States would again project military strength abroad.

Although the US Jewish reaction to Reagan's election in November 1979 was not enthusiastic, it was entirely different in Israel. The fact that a

candidate with strong pro-Israel credentials defeated Carter was merely icing on the cake; more important was the relief of being rid of a president (Carter) they had long ceased viewing with anything but distrust. They were equally pleased to bid adieu to the Carter foreign policy team, particularly Carter's National Security Adviser, Zbigniew Brzezinski.

Zbigniew Brzezinski

The same responses were echoed again in 2016 with the startling upset election of Donald J. Trump. Yogi Berra would have rightly pointed out that it must have seemed like, *"deja vu* all over again!"

Lawrence Peter "Yogi" Berra (1925 –2015) was an American professional baseball catcher, who later took on the roles of manager and coach. He is widely regarded as one of the greatest catchers in baseball history, and was elected to the Baseball Hall of Fame in 1972. Berra quit school after the eighth grade. He was known for his malapropisms as well as pithy and paradoxical statements, such as *"It ain't over 'til it's over"*, while speaking to reporters. He once  simultaneously denied and confirmed his reputation by stating, *"I really didn't say everything I said.*

In 2016, the Israeli fear of a Hillary Clinton White House built on the foundations of the Obama-Kerry Wrecking Crew was just too much to contemplate for another four years. The pleasant shock of the brash and rash New York business tycoon surrounded by Jewish family and advisors gave Israel hope for better US relations, just as the arrival of the Hollywood actor did some 35 years before. Some Israelis even jokingly called the Trumpian descent on an escalator to announce his candidacy as a "second coming."

Why the US Stands with Israel From Moral to Strategic Reasons

During the first seven years of the Reagan administration, US official support for the state of Israel shifted significantly from the prevailing moral reasoning toward strategic justifications. This shift in the official rhetoric was accompanied by concrete policy moves tying the militaries of the two countries much closer together than ever before.

The shift in US declaratory policy described as Israel's strategic worth to the United States, did not initially start with the Reagan administration, but it was greatly intensified during those years.
The Israelis now positively contributed to US security: their combat experience and capture of Russian equipment provided information important to the American military in Vietnam.

Israel's new conservative republican sympathizers were more likely than its previous liberal supporters to agree with a military approach to conducting foreign policy and with the need for advanced weaponry.
The changing policy had its start long before the Reagan days.
It started when Lyndon Johnson secretly approved an increased exchange of intelligence with the Israelis.

Oddly enough it was after the tragic affair of the strafing of the American USS *Liberty*.

The USS *LIBERTY* AFFAIR

During the Six-Day War, on June 8, 1967, Israeli war planes and torpedo boats attacked the USS *Liberty,* a signals intelligence gathering ship on a collections mission in international waters off the Sinai Peninsula. Thirty-four US sailors died and 171 were injured in the attack.

Left: Israeli torpedo boats; center and right: damage to the USS *Liberty*

There are many theories attempting to explain the horrific confrontation between allies. Many of the theories standing alone appear to have credibility as to how it happened but fail to adequately explain why a friendly ally (in a world where Israel doesn't have many friends) would attack a US Navy ship. After reading many of the explanations and charges that all border on conspiracy theories, I've tentatively concluded that the simplest explanation is probably closest to the truth. This line of reasoning known as 'Occam's Razor, is the process of shaving down stacks of information based on suppositions to make finding the truth easier. The old Franciscan friar, William of Occam might have stated it this way, "The simplest answer is most often the correct answer."

William of Ockham c. 1287 – 1347 was an English Franciscan friar, scholastic philosopher, and theologian, who is believed to have been born in Ockham, a small village in Surrey. He is considered to be one of the major figures of medieval thought and was at the centre of the major intellectual and political controversies of the 14th century. He is commonly known for **Occam's Razor,** the methodological principle that bears his name, and also produced significant works on logic, physics, and theology.

It is quite possible that what happened to the USS Liberty was just what the Israeli and US governments publicly concluded it was, a tragic accident in the fog of war. It wouldn't be the first time that multiple human errors culminated in a terrible tragedy.

Less than six months later, in early 1968, the Israelis even stepped up their requests for US military technology. This was hardly the action of a chastised and guilty party. To argue their case for Johnson's approval of the sale of Phantom (F-4) fighter planes, their former IDF Chief of Staff, Yitzhak Rabin was sent as Ambassador to Washington.
That appointment symbolized the change in the relationship of the two allies.

In October of 1968, even though the US was deeply mired in Vietnam, Johnson approved the Phantom sale. Amidst the pro-Israeli rhetoric generated by the U.S. presidential election of that year, Johnson asked no quid pro quo such as Israeli withdrawal from the occupied Arab areas, or Israeli agreement to sign the Nuclear Non-proliferation Treaty, both being urged by his Secretary of State Dean Rusk and Defense Secretary Clark Clifford.

A decade later, in August of 1979, presidential candidate Reagan wrote about, "Israel's geopolitical importance as a . . . "military offset to the Soviet Union," and of its value, "as perhaps the only remaining strategic asset in the region on which the United States can truly rely."
The future president concluded that, "Only by full appreciation of the critical role the State of Israel plays in our strategic calculus can we build the foundation for thwarting Moscow's designs on territories and resources vital to our security and our national wellbeing."

> **"If we ever forget that we are One Nation Under God, then we will be a nation gone under." Reagan**

Anyone who followed the public political career of the former actor had little doubt about his pro-Israel views. He denounced the PLO as a terrorist organization and described Israel as a "strategic asset," a "stabilizing force," and a military offset to Soviet influence.

Throughout the campaign, Reagan made a point of differentiating his views on Israel from those of President Carter. As he reminded Jewish audiences, he had been appalled by the Carter Administration's decision to abstain rather than veto a UN resolution condemning Israel's proclamation of Jerusalem as its capital.

"Jerusalem is now, and should continue to be, undivided," declared Reagan. *"An undivided city of Jerusalem means sovereignty of Israel over the city."*

He also publicly disagreed with the Carter Administration's efforts to characterize Israel's West Bank settlements as illegal and was quick to reaffirm this position shortly after the election.

If Reagan came to those conclusions in 1980, why did it take nearly two decades to put them into action under Trump? Maybe the two major political parties weren't really that different after all.

While researching this chapter on Reagan, I came to the amazing conclusion that Reagan's policies after coming into office were very much in line with his pre-election rhetoric. This theme was strongly evident throughout the first years of his administration. He was the first president that I remembered who actually kept his electioneering promises. What a shock! He even referred to "Promises made and kept."

164

Reagan's First Secretary of State

Alexander M. Haig, Reagan's choice for Secretary of State (1981-1982), was definitely the most pro-Israel advocate in his first cabinet. Haig's first goal in the Middle East was the creation of an American-Israeli-Arab 'strategic consensus' that would confront the Soviet Union's attempts to re-enter the region. When it became clear that the Arabs would not enter into such an arrangement alongside Israel, and that they gave priority to regional, rather than East-West threats, Haig became the architect of the bilateral US-Israeli 'Memorandum of Understanding (MOU) on strategic cooperation that was concluded in November 1981.

Haig likened Israel's strategic location and reliability as America's most substantial ally as a friendly nation taking the place of "the largest American aircraft carrier in the world that cannot be sunk, does not carry even one American soldier, and is located in a critical region for American national security."

Haig had served as Chief of Staff in the Nixon White House during Israel's 1973 Yom Kippur War. When it became known that Israel was losing tanks at an alarming rate, the former general cut across many Departments and bureaucratic roadblocks endemic to the DC swamp. Haig knew that the US recently had developed a new and superior anti-tank missile, which Israel needed desperately, with no authorization Haig not only shipped the weapons to Israel but trained IDF troops in the use of those weapons. Haig rushed to the defense of Israel and only after the fact did President Nixon authorize the official aid.

Although in 2001 Haig had long been out of government, he kept current on Middle Eastern events by heading up a consulting firm.
He told a *Washington Post* reporter that it might be a good thing for Israel to stop Iran from becoming a nuclear power.
"If the Israelis do launch a preemptive strike [on Iran], it may be saving the world a lot of trouble," he said in his unique understated manner of speaking.

165

Had anyone listened to Haig, whom the press often likened to a 'bumbling illiterate' by labeling his rhetoric as "Haigspeak" the world would not still be facing the Iranian nuclear threat decades later.

"Haigspeak"

Alexander Haig was the second of three career military officers to become secretary of state (George C. Marshall and Colin Powell were the others). His speeches in this role in particular led to the coining of the neologism "Haigspeak," described in a dictionary of neologisms as "Language characterized by pompous obscurity resulting from redundancy, the semantically strained use of words, and verbosity," leading Ambassador Nicko Henderson to offer a prize for the best rendering of the Gettysburg address in Haigspeak"."

Reagan's First United Nation's Ambassador

To represent the United States at the United Nations, Reagan chose **Jeane J. Kirkpatrick.**
In 1982 she described herself as, "a very good friend of Israel", reassuring her American Jewish audience that, "There are a good many of us throughout the administration, beginning at the top."

Kirkpatrick shared Reagan's belief, reiterated throughout the 1980 campaign, that "Resolutions in the United Nations which undermine Israel's positions and isolate her people should be vetoed because they undermine progress toward peace."

Only the newly appointed U.S. Ambassador to the United Nations Jeanne J. Kirkpatrick stood in the way of an anti-Israel vote. Realizing that the word "aggression" had terrible consequences for Israel as it would make it appear that the attack was unprovoked and that the attacked party, Iraq, might now legitimately undertake unspecified self-defense measures, she strenuously argued that the U.S. should abstain from voting for that resolution, unless the word "aggression" was deleted. In the end, after taking the matter directly to President Reagan, her efforts prevailed, and "aggression" was deleted from the resolution allowing the US to half-heartedly join in the condemnation. This set the tone for much that was to follow at the UN during the years of the Reagan presidency.

Reagan's First Secretary of Defense

By all accounts, the sole dissenter as to the importance of the US-Israel partytnership at the cabinet level was Secretary of Defense **Caspar Weinberger.** He wasn't soft on the core issue of the Soviet threat. His views on the Jewish state were reinforced by the deeply entrenched institutional and bureaucratic wisdom within the Defense and State Departments. They believed that countries such as Turkey, Egypt and Saudi Arabia, with their populations and military size, could make a much  greater contribution to sustaining the US defense posture and opposition to the Soviets in the Middle East than Israel was able to.

During the Reagan years, Weinberger's anti-Israel tilt was an underlying current in almost every Mideast issue. Some said it was because of his years with the Bechtel Corporation. Others believed it had to do with his sensitivity about his own Jewish ancestry. As an Episcopalian, whose paternal grandparents converted to Christianity, Weinberger's personal feelings about Jews and Judaism certainly were "complicated" and extremely sensitive.

In his biography *In the Arena*, Weinberger bluntly laid to rest the assumption that he was raised Jewish. Both his father and grandfather had become indifferent to any religion because of a synagogue quarrel in Bohemia three generations earlier. However, when asked about why he lost his bid to become California State Attorney General. Weinberger responded, "Because the Jews knew I wasn't Jewish and the Gentiles thought I was."
Because of his surname, he always stressed that he was not Jewish.

Weinberger with Ariel Sharon

During his Secretary of Defense position (from 1981 to 1987), he visited Israel for the first time. At Yad Vashem, Israel's Holocaust museum, his guide, who was a prosecutor in the trial against Adolf Eichmann, told him, "If you had been in Germany at that time, this would have happened to you, too."
To which Weinberger retorted in a loud voice, "I am not a Jew!"

Reagan Nearly Assassinated

Only 70 days into the new administration, on March 30, 1981, the president was struck by gunfire from would-be assassin John Hinckley Jr. outside the Washington Hilton Hotel. Although "close to death" upon arrival at George Washington University Hospital, the Reagan humor remained intact as he looked at the surgeons and quipped, *"Please tell me you're all Republicans."*
In early April the recovered president was released from the hospital.

He was the first serving US president to survive an assassination attempt. Reagan believed that God had spared his life so that he might go on to fulfill a greater purpose.

Strategic Cooperation With Israel

Reagan became the first American president to formally authorize the signing of a "Strategic Cooperation Agreement" between the United States and Israel. Its goal was to thwart greater Soviet influence in the Middle East and affirm his Administration's intention of enhancing Israel's special relationship with the United States. During Reagan's time in the White House no corresponding strategic pact was signed with any Arab state.

America's financial aid to Israel steadily increased throughout the Reagan years. Beginning in 1986, it reached an unprecedented $3 billion a year, in loans and grants. More than three decades later the amount of US aid to Israel has not significantly increased on an annual dollar basis.

During Reagan's years a great percentage of the aid was for economic assistance. Today, it is mainly in Foreign Military Financing. It includes joint development projects, especially in missile and anti-ballistic systems where the United States is a partner and a benefactor of the new systems.

Even the purchase of US-made fighter planes is of a financial benefit to the US because Israel helps keep our production lines open which benefits our own workforce and overall economy. Israeli pilots, also stationed in the American manufacturing plants, receive daily reports on the combat capabilities and needs of the US-made aircraft. This improves the product and makes it more attractive to other foreign nations to purchase.

Israel's three newest F-35 stealth fighter jets on their way to Israel in April 2017.

What was seen in the past as "foreign aid giveaways" is now, in Israel's case, a viable "investment with guaranteed payoffs".

Israel not only has become a strategic partner but also an economic business partner.

I won't bore you readers with a row of figures that prove my point, but as the "Old Professor" Casey Stengel used to say, *"Youse guys could look it up."*

Charles Dillon "Casey" Stengel (1890 – 1975) was an American Major League Baseball right fielder and manager, best known as the manager of the championship New York Yankees of the 1950s and later the New York Mets. He was elected to the Baseball Hall of Fame in 1966. Stengel had become famous for his humorous and sometimes disjointed way of speech while with the Yankees. The "Old Perfesser" is remembered as one of the great characters in baseball history.

The First big Bump on the Road to Strategic Cooperation

The Reagan administration's path toward the establishment of strategic links with Israel did not always go smoothly.

A big bump on the road occurred on the 7th of June 1981. Israeli F-16s, recently acquired from the United States, bombed Saddam Hussein's Iraqi nuclear facility in Iraq, in apparent contravention of US legislation governing arms transfers abroad. That successful yet startling attack on the Iraqi reactor at Osirak, near Baghdad, caused a big problem. The meticulously planned operation came as a complete surprise to the Reagan administration as it did to the Iraqis. The unprecedented Israeli attack, code named "Operation Opera", earned its place in the highest level of Combat Aviation History. For the most part, it had been a relatively conventional low-level interdiction air strike. One of several things that made Operation Opera sensational was the audacity of Israel for launching the strike, an aggressive act that Israel would have to defend with vigor for years to come.

Operation Opera also known as **Operation Babylon**, was a surprise Israeli air strike carried out on 7 June 1981 which destroyed an Iraqi nuclear reactor under construction 17 kilometers (10.5 miles) southeast of Baghdad. The operation came after Iran's unsuccessful Operation Scorch Sword had caused minor damage to the same nuclear facility the previous year, the damage having been subsequently repaired by French technicians.

Operation Opera, and related Israeli government statements following it, established the **Begin Doctrine,** which explicitly stated the strike was not an anomaly, but instead "a precedent for every future government in Israel."

Israel's counter-proliferation preventive strike added another dimension to their existing policy of deliberate ambiguity as it related to the nuclear capability of other states in the region.

On 7 June 1981, a flight of Israeli Air Force F-16A fighter aircraft, with an escort of F-15As, bombed and heavily damaged the Osirak reactor. Israel called the operation an act of self-defense and said that the reactor had "less than a month to go" before "it might have become critical." Ten Iraqi soldiers and one French civilian were killed.

At the time, the attack was met with sharp international criticism, including in the United States, and Israel was rebuked by the United Nations Security Council and General Assembly in two separate resolutions.

Media reactions were also negative: "Israel's sneak attack ... was an act of inexcusable and short-sighted aggression", wrote the New York Times, while the Los Angeles Times called it "state-sponsored terrorism".
The destruction of Osirak has been cited as an example of a preventive strike in contemporary scholarship on international law. The efficacy of the attack is debated by historians, who acknowledge that it brought back Iraq from the brink of nuclear capability but drove its weapons program underground and cemented Saddam Hussein's future ambitions for acquiring nuclear weapons.

Operation Opera

The Israelis chose to use eight lightweight, single-engine F-16As as the bomb-carrying strike aircraft and assigned six of the heavier, twin engine F-15 aircraft to fly combat air cover over the attack aircraft.

Ilan Ramon's F-16A

En-route to the target, the Israeli planes crossed the gulf of Aqaba.

Unknowingly, the squadron flew directly over the yacht of King Hussein of Jordan, who was vacationing in the Gulf at the time. The king himself an accomplished pilot, noticed the Israeli markings on the planes overflying his yacht. Taking into account the location, heading, and armament on the jets, Hussein quickly figured that the Iraqi reactor was the most probable target. The Jordanian king immediately contacted his government and ordered a warning to be sent to the Iraqis.

However, due to a communication failure the message was never received.

The flight was detected and questioned by Jordanian air controllers. An Israeli pilot responded in Saudi-accented Arabic that they were from the Saudi Air Force and had made a miscalculation and would soon be going home. Another enemy sighting was dismissed when this closely packed formation of 14 planes was thought to be a jumbo jet which was temporarily off course. Nevertheless, this low flying attack group had exhausted the fuel in their external fuel pods and had to eject them into the desert sands. (No camels or other animals were hurt in the making of this mission...)

172

Upon reaching Iraqi airspace the squadron split up, with two of the F-15s forming close escort to the F-16 squadron, and the remaining F-15s dispersing into Iraqi airspace as a diversion and a ready back-up. In an attempt to fly under the radar of the Iraqi defenses, the attack squadron descended to 100 feet over the Iraqi desert. Just before the attack, the radar of the anti-aircraft batteries shut down as the crews went to dinner. The attack was planned for Sunday on the presumption that the French nuclear workers would have the day off and not be on site to mitigate the possibility of killing French nationalists in the raid.

It took less than two minutes for the eight Israeli F-16 fighter bombers to destroy the Osirak reactor that was located 18 miles south of Baghdad. The 70-megawatt uranium-powered reactor was near completion but had not yet been stocked with nuclear fuel. According to sources in the French atomic industry there was no danger of a radiation leak.

"The future doesn't belong to the fainthearted; it belongs to the brave."

Reagan

After the 2,000 mile, three-hour mission, all the aircraft were safely back at their base. None of the planes were damaged, but they had landed on fumes. The next morning none of the aircraft were able to start, such was the extreme usage of the machines on an un-refueled mission that was universally believed to have been practically impossible.

Most of the Israeli army, air force, Mossad, and political leadership had

been opposed to the audacious plan. It was only the steely will and foresight of Prime Minister **Menachem Begin** that saw the imminent existential threat to the Jewish state. He took the initiative to order the attack. Even today, many believe that this was one of the greatest decisions made by a world leader in ensuring the survivability of his nation. Because of his unflinching courage and right-wing politics, he was never given the respect that he deserved while he was alive.

President Reagan initially shrugged off the daring attack in surprised but quiet admiration of Israel's initiative aggressiveness, and *chutzpah.*

That Sunday afternoon, the President was climbing into a helicopter at Camp David when he was reached in an urgent phone call by his National Security Adviser and informed of the raid on Iraq. At first Reagan fell silent, and the only sound the NSA heard was the churning of the copter.

Reagan's classic response was heard, "Well... boys will be boys!"

This was typical Reagan. While recognizing the long-range strategic consequences and realizing the seriousness of the situation, he could also cut to the chase with a pithy off-the-cuff comment. It was very much like Abraham Lincoln used to do one hundred twenty years before.

However, in his diary on the night of 7 June, the President voiced a more extreme pessimism: *"I swear I believe Armageddon is near."*

During the next National Security Council meeting, negative opinions against Israel's action were presented by vice president George H. W. Bush, Chief of Staff James Baker and the president's aide, Michael Deaver.

The "Troika." From left: James Baker, Ed Meese* , Michael Deaver. These men were known as the Troika" because of their vast influence during the Reagan presidency. Ed Meese did not voice his concerns during the Security meeting, but Bush did.

President Reagan and vice president George H. W. Bush

"One picture is worth
1,000 denials."
Reagan

175

They argued strongly for punitive actions against Israel, including taking back aircraft and delaying or canceling scheduled deliveries. On the other hand, they received the unexpected news that several important Middle East countries, while publicly professing outrage and dismay, were privately pleased.

Given his well-known animosity toward Israel, no one was surprised that Secretary of Defense Caspar Weinberger was angry. Secretary of State Alexander Haig carefully presented the diplomatic concerns. Before the meeting, Haig was inclined to stand more verbally behind Israel, but great pressure from within the State Department and from other countries prompted him to be less vocal and ultimately to authorize official American criticism of Israel.

Reagan journaled in his diary,
"Begin insists the plant was preparing to produce nuclear weapons for use on Israel. If he waited 'til the French shipment of "hot" uranium arrived he couldn't order the bombing because the radiation that would be loosed over Baghdad. I can understand his fear but feel he took the wrong option…. However, we are not turning on Israel - that would be an invitation for the Arabs to attack."

Europe chimed in with France declaring it "unacceptable";
Britain denounced it as "a grave breach of international law."
A *New York Times* editorial began: "Israel's sneak attack on a French-built nuclear reactor near Baghdad was an act of inexcusable and short-sighted aggression."

The Carter Double-cross

In retrospect, the condemnations were completely wrong. Later it was discovered that former President **Jimmy Carter** had been in significant consultation with Israel about the existential threat from Iraqi dictator Saddam Hussein's nuclear reactor. In fact, it was Carter who had left Reagan out of the loop when briefing the incoming president about our ally's capabilities and plans.

Carter, the former American president, was poisoning the well of the American government against Begin and his Likud Party.

The 16th of June entry in the president's diary confirmed that the Carter administration had "forgotten" to brief the impending attack to the new president.

"We have just learned that Israel & the previous Admin. did communicate about Iraq & the nuclear threat and the U.S. agreed it was a threat. There was never a mention of this to us by the outgoing admin. Amb. Lewis cabled word to us after the Israeli attack on Iraq & now we find there was a stack of cables & memos tucked away in St. Dept. files."

Reagan and Begin

The preventive strike on Iraq and other unilateral actions effectively introduced a policy that was later called "The Begin Doctrine". This proclaimed the idea that Israel would undertake military action to prevent the development of external threats by its Middle Eastern adversaries. The Osirak attack and the other manifestation of the Begin Doctrine—including the 2007 Operation "Outside the Box" attack against the Syrian nuclear site—have repeatedly been cited as examples of the right of anticipatory self-defense (pre-emptive strike), which enables countries to strike potential foes while not under immediate threat.

Operation "Outside the Box" was an Israeli airstrike on a suspected nuclear reactor, referred to as the Al Kibar site (Dair Alzour), in Syria, around midnight (local time) on 6 September 2007. The site was a known nuclear facility with a military purpose, which Syria denied.

When U.S. President George W.

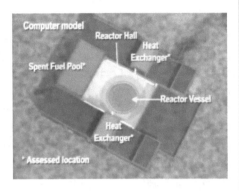

Bush was unwilling to bomb the facility, Prime Minister Ehud Olmert decided to adhere to the 1981 Begin Doctrine and unilaterally strike to prevent a Syrian nuclear weapons capability, despite serious concerns about Syrian retaliation. This airstrike did not elicit international outcry (like the one on the Osirak reactor) because Israel maintained total and complete silence regarding the attack, and Syria covered up its activities at the site and did not cooperate fully with the IAEA.

According to official government confirmation on 21 March 2018, the raid was carried out by Israeli Air Force (IAF) 69 Squadron F-15Is, and 119 Squadron and 253 Squadron F-16Is, and an ELINT aircraft; as many as eight aircraft participated and at least four of these crossed into Syrian airspace. The fighters were equipped with AGM-65 Maverick missiles, 500 lb bombs, and external fuel tanks.

69 Squadron F151

The attack pioneered the use of Israel's electronic warfare capabilities, as IAF electronic warfare (EW) systems took over Syria's air defense systems, feeding them a false sky-picture for the entire period of time that the Israeli fighter jets needed to cross Syria, bomb their target and return.

Reactor before and after

A decade later, in 1991, then Secretary of Defense **Dick Cheney** praised the "outstanding" Israeli operation for "making our job much easier in Desert Storm." Ten years earlier, however, American officials had a much different take on Operation Opera.

Thank God that Menachem Begin overrode his own intelligence agency and the fears of most of his advisors who worried that the attack would affect the peace process with Egypt and Israel's already shaky position in the U.N. He did what any righteous world leader must do - first and foremost protect his own nation by destroying the capabilities of an enemy bent on his nation's destruction.

Over time, and particularly in light of Iraqi aggression against Kuwait in 1990, the international community has viewed the Osirak strike in a more positive and reasonable light.

In the aftermath of the 1981 Osirak strike, the Reagan administration was put on the defensive. In an effort to assuage Arab anger, it suspended the delivery of six F-16 aircraft to Israel and voted in support of a UN Security Council resolution condemning the raid, infuriating Israeli officials who insisted that they had acted in self-defense.

The administration doubled down on a controversial arms package to Saudi Arabia in the early fall, provoking a bruising congressional battle that deepened the gulf between Washington and Jerusalem.

As a result, the Reagan administration's influence over Israel's foreign policies weakened at a crucial time for Israel. Prime Minister Begin embarked on a series of dramatic military operations, including the

bombing of PLO headquarters in Beirut in July 1981, the annexation of the Golan Heights in December 1981, and the sudden invasion of Lebanon in June 1982—all of which heightened tensions and weakened the United States' position in the region.

1981 Begin's visit to the White House

179

The biggest lesson from the Osirak attack may have been that international condemnation doesn't have much long-term impact. After the attack, Israel shrugged off widespread criticism, while Iraq largely ignored international nonproliferation obligations. Indeed, over time the Osirak strike became "respectable," and generally viewed as an appropriate response to the threat posed by Saddam's regime.

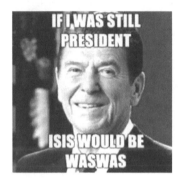

Today, the legitimacy of the strike is seldom questioned, which has probably made it easier for the United States and others to think about military action in preventive terms. This precedent may possibly play a large role in the future legal justification for possible US strikes against nuclear threats in Iran and even North Korea.

The Next Bumps in the Road Came Fast and Furious

Despite the Osirak bump in the road, an unprecedented Memorandum of Understanding (MOU) was painstakingly drawn up between the USA and Israel.

US-Israel Memorandum of Understanding, 30 Oct 1981

Memorandum of Understanding between the Government of the United States and the Government of Israel on Strategic Cooperation November 30, 1981. After a few weeks of discussions between working groups, Israel's Defense Minister Sharon and the U.S. Defense Secretary Weinberger signed on 30 November in Washington a memorandum of understanding on strategic cooperation. The main objective was to deter Soviet threats in the Middle East. There would be joint military exercises, land, sea and air; there would also be planning for the establishment and maintenance of joint readiness activities. Joint working teams will deal with specific military issues. The Arab world and the Soviet Union were highly critical of this agreement, which they felt would impair America's ability to deal fairly with the peace process in the Middle East. This memorandum of understanding reaffirms the common bonds of friendship between the United States and Israel and builds on the mutual security relationship that exists between the two nations. The parties recognize the need to enhance strategic cooperation to deter all threats from the Soviet Union to the region. Noting the longstanding and fruitful cooperation for mutual security that has developed between the two countries, the parties have decided to establish a framework for continued consultation and cooperation to enhance their national security by deterring such threats to the whole region

In an interview broadcast by Jerusalem radio the next morning, Israeli Defense minister Sharon stated that, "Some American supporters of the MOU hope that its conclusion might help to rein Israel in from taking the kind of rash actions that could de-stabilize American interests in the Middle East."

Ariel Sharon and Menachem Begin

It was hoped that the new strategic MOU would usher in a new era of cooperation and security. But it was not to be.

Two weeks later on December 14 of 1981, Prime Minister Begin introduced a resolution in the Israeli Knesset that extended Israeli law to the occupied Golan Heights. Four days after the resolution was

passed, the State Department announced the suspension—but not the cancellation—of the MOU.

Begin's counter-response was tough. Calling in US Ambassador Samuel Lewis, he read him the Israeli version of the riot act by demanding, "What kind of talk is this, 'punishing Israel'? Are we a vassal state of yours? Are we a banana republic?"

Begin and Lewis

Thus ended the first phase of formal strategic cooperation. However, once the dust had settled from the Golan affair, relations soon improved, and Israel got most of what it wanted through that agreement.

Similarly, when it came to Arab efforts to characterize East Jerusalem as "occupied territory," President Reagan instructed his delegates to the UN to veto such resolutions on the grounds that the final status on Jerusalem was to be negotiated (thanks to LBJ and Arthur Goldberg and their work on UN Resolution 242) and not subject to resolution by legal fiat.

> "Freedom is never more than one generation away from extinction. We didn't pass it to our children in the bloodstream. It must be fought for, protected, and handed on for them to do the same."
>
> **Reagan**

The Reagan and Gorbachev Summits Open the Gates

During that stormy time in 1981, no one would have guessed that ten years later Reagan's efforts would have been the catalyst that opened the flood gates of the Soviet Union for the million plus "Russian brain DRAIN." Which ushered in an "Israeli Brain GAIN" into the very head and heart of the Jewish State. This Brain Gain would transform it into a technological giant labeled "Silicon Wadi" rivaling California's "Silicon Valley."

Certain issues were very close to Reagan's heart. As a private citizen, he had become aware of the Soviet war on religion. The Soviet leadership was an equal opportunity discriminator, attacking religious believers of all stripes. In fact, Communists everywhere assaulted religious believers: in the USSR, Romania, China, Cambodia, Cuba, etc. Reagan noticed that Jews in particular had suffered cruel persecution under Communism. "Even the Sandinistas in Nicaragua," said Reagan, "had used threats and harassment to force virtually every Nicaraguan Jew to flee the country."

Even though Soviet Jews could apply for exit visas, the vast majority were denied. First, the 'refusenik' would lose his or her job. In the Soviet Union, where it was illegal to be without a job, they were now accused of parasitism. As punishment for wanting to leave their glorious Motherland, the Soviet government would now assign world-renowned scientists a menial job like a street sweeper or elevator operator. In 1984, the number of Jews allowed to leave Russia was down to 896, the lowest point in modern Jewish emigration history. When Gorbachev entered the office in March 1985, there were over 11,000 Jews listed as "refuseniks". Thousands of other Jews were in jail or labor camps for the crimes of either learning Hebrew or applying to emigrate.

> **"How can a President not be an actor?"**
> **Reagan**

January 10, 1973. Soviet Jewish refuseniks demonstrate in front of the Ministry of Internal Affairs for the right to emigrate to Israel.

Reagan was determined to help those Jews. In fact, he always carried an updated list of imprisoned refuseniks in his coat pocket.

Each time Secretary of State **George Shultz** prepared to travel to the USSR or to meet with his Soviet counterpart, Reagan would pull out "the list" and say, "George, I want you to raise these names with the Soviets."

Sure enough, Shultz would raise them and one by one, they would be released from the Gulag and often even allowed to leave the country. Most of them were Jews like Anatoly "Natan" Sharansky, who had suffered nine years of imprisonment for daring to request permission to leave for Israel. He was released in 1986. Natan Sharansky eventually became the head of Israel's Jewish Agency and a world-renowned figure in pushing for the eventual release of millions from the grasp of Communism.

Reagan Bugs Gorbachev About the Soviet Jews Five Times

On December 6, 1987, some 250,000 Jews came together on the National Mall in Washington, DC, to protest on behalf of Soviet Jewry. The demonstration, one day ahead of the Washington summit between Reagan and Gorbachev, called for freedom of emigration for the millions of Soviet Jews, as well as an end to their persecution within the Communist bloc.

Sharansky, released from the Gulag one year earlier, said, "[Gorbachev] was releasing one after another prisoner of Zion, [but] it was still a limited number, in order to decrease the pressure without opening the gates. After this demonstration it was absolutely clear that nothing less than releasing Soviet Jews and bringing down the Iron Curtain will satisfy America. They could not compromise on anything less than freedom of immigration."

Among the speakers was then vice president George H.W. Bush. In his speech, he echoed the words of Reagan at the Berlin Wall in June, "Mr. Gorbachev," he said, "Let these people go. Let them go."

Reagan did not merely act through intermediaries but sometimes took his demands to the highest level. General Secretary Gorbachev found

out the moment he arrived at the White House on December 8, to commence the third summit in three years between the United States and the USSR.

After the welcoming ceremony, he and Reagan and their interpreters went to the Oval Office. Reagan seized on the one-on-one session to hammer the issue of Soviet human-rights violations. Even though he was pleased that some Soviet Jews were being permitted to leave the Soviet Union, Reagan felt more should be allowed. As he had at Geneva and Reykjavik, Gorbachev bristled when he heard the translation of Reagan's remarks on human rights. Reagan recalled the general secretary's sensitive reaction: "He replied that he was not the accused standing in a dock, and I was not a prosecutor, and that I had no right to bring up domestic matters of the Soviet Union."

Gorbachev was always perturbed by Reagan's insistence on open emigration for Soviet Jews. Still angry a decade later, Gorbachev recalled in his memoirs how he snapped at Reagan: "Mr. President, like you, I represent a great country and therefore expect our dialogue to be conducted on the basis of reciprocity and equality. Otherwise there simply will be no dialogue."

Yet, Reagan continued to speak about the necessity of letting the Jews go. His opening remarks, which seemed to go on forever, frustrated Gorbachev more and more. When Reagan finally moved on to the agreed upon agenda items, he was confident that the dialogue on the Jews would continue. They did, during the next summit, six months later in Moscow.

The May 1989 meeting of the two world leaders was the fifth and last meeting between them as heads of state. Their first one-on-one meeting began at 3:26 p.m., Sunday, May 29, 1988. It lasted an hour and 11 minutes. Gorbachev began the conversation, and when it was Reagan's turn, he immediately began speaking on religion in Russia. He spoke of Jews, Muslims, Protestants, and Ukrainian Catholics, and insisted all had a right to attend the place of worship of their choice.

Gorbachev responded by claiming that in Russia there was no religion problem. The debate continued. Reagan's next bold move revealed his priorities: he linked Gorbachev's economic demands to his own personal goal of religious freedom in the USSR.

"Gorbachev again expressed his desire for increased U.S.-Soviet trade," recalled Reagan later. "I was ready for him."

Here was Reagan, at the top of his game, telling Gorbachev: "One reason we have trouble increasing trade with your country is because of Soviet human rights abuses." Again, he singled out religious freedom, "I'm not trying to tell you how to run your country," he told Gorbachev, "but I realize you are probably concerned that if you allow too many of the Jews who want to emigrate from the Soviet Union to leave, there'll be a 'brain drain,' a loss of skilled people from your economy. But did it ever occur to you, on this whole question of human rights, that maybe if the Jews were permitted to worship as they want to and teach their children the Hebrew language, that maybe they wouldn't want to leave the Soviet Union? Perhaps, if they were allowed to reopen their synagogues and worship as they want to, they might decide that they wouldn't have to leave and there wouldn't be that problem of a brain drain."

As to the effect of this on Gorbachev, Reagan later recorded in his diary:

"Whether my words had any impact or not I don't know, but after that the Soviet government began allowing more churches and synagogues to reopen."

An October 6, 1988 statement from the Moscow Domestic Service accused Reagan of turning to the issue of Jewish emigration "whenever it has been necessary to open another anti-Soviet, anti-socialist campaign."

The Soviets were annoyed because Reagan once again had the audacity to decry the continued persecution of Soviet Jews.

"President Reagan said in his speech that there are tens and perhaps hundreds of thousands of Jews in the USSR who long for exit visas and are not getting them," complained Moscow. *"Who has felt this need to appeal to figures that have clearly been dreamed up and plucked from thin air and wrap them in tendentious rhetoric?"*

"Why," the Moscow Domestic Service went on, *"is he once again trying to whip up passions and blow up nonexistent problems?"*

In the next line, Moscow provided an answer: *"Perhaps this is to the advantage of the Zionist circles which are trying to distract the attention of the world public in this way from the genocide that they themselves are perpetrating against the Palestinians in the Israeli occupied Arab lands? It's no accident that in the same speech, President Reagan allowed himself an outburst against the United Nations, which in his opinion ought to rescind Resolution 3379, passed in 1975, which describes Zionism as a form of racial discrimination."*

In 1989, Soviet President Mikhail Gorbachev finally decided to lift restrictions on emigration. That same year, 71,000 Soviet Jews emigrated, of whom only 12,117 immigrated to Israel.

However, in October 1989, the US government stopped treating Soviet Jews as refugees, because Israel was willing to accept them unconditionally. In 1990, 183,400 Soviet immigrants arrived in Israel. Approximately 148,000 more arrived in 1991.

Between 1992 and 1995, immigration to Israel from the former Soviet Union averaged around 70,000 per year.

As the wave of emigration began, Soviet Jews wanting to emigrate left the Soviet Union for various European transit points from which they were flown to Israel. The Israeli government ordered the national airline El Al to put every available plane at the disposal of the immigrants. Some Soviet immigrants also came by sea on chartered ships.

The first direct flight to Israel with 125 immigrants departed Moscow on January 1, 1990. Eventually, every city in the former Soviet Union with a large Jewish population became a staging point for direct flights to Tel Aviv.

When President Reagan left the office on January 20, 1989, the Berlin Wall was still intact and most of the Soviet Jews were still imprisoned. Eventually, Ronald Reagan succeeded even beyond his wildest dreams. The Berlin Wall came down in 1989, the USSR imploded in 1991, and the Cold War was over. Liberation for millions of people was achieved without the horrible nuclear exchange so many had feared.

At long last, Soviet Jews finally had the right to leave. Many streamed into Israel in the largest exodus since the founding of the modern Israeli State and the escape from the Egyptian Pharaoh.

By mid-1990's, when Reagan's mind was being consumed by Alzheimer's disease, he thankfully still was able to comprehend the tremendous accomplishment.

By 1997, however, his disease was progressing fast and the White House, the Soviets, and all those suffering behind the Iron Curtain had become flickering memories.

That summer, Ronald Reagan received a meaningful thank you while strolling through Armand Hammer Park near his Bel Air home.

A tourist, Yakov Ravin and his twelve-year-old grandson, approached him. The Jewish Ukrainian immigrants cheered Reagan as he drew near and briefly spoke to him. The grandfather then proudly snapped a picture of the retired president with his grandson. "Mr. President," said Ravin, "thank you for everything you did for the Jewish people, for Soviet people, to destroy the communist empire." Slightly confused, 86-year-old Reagan responded: "Yes, that is my job." That was his job. And many longed

to thank him.

Most never did, at least not to his face. Instead, many thousands came out in the immediate days after June 5, 2004, when Reagan died at the age of 93.

Some AP reporters interviewed

Rabbi **Velvel Tsikman** – one of the upwards of 50,000 Soviet bloc immigrants living today in the greater Los Angeles area – who remembered a time when the only link he had to his Jewish heritage was a line in his Soviet passport that read: "Nationality: Jewish."

In the USSR, Rabbi Tsikman was forbidden to wear a yarmulke. Now, he leads a vibrant Russian Jewish community in West Hollywood from his office at the Chabad Russian Jewish Community Center.

Rabbi Tsikman

And he credits his spiritual freedom to Ronald Reagan.

"[Reagan's] doctrine," said Rabbi Tsikman, "what he did, was very helpful to destroy the monster that was there in Europe."

Rabbi Tsikman spoke about the elderly people in the retirement center

who left the USSR late in life. "They are living in a paradise here," he said. "It's like God is paying them for a terrible life in Russia. These people were sitting at home, waiting to die. When they came here, they came alive again."

If Ronald Reagan were alive

The 'old' life for Russian Jews

today, he would be thrilled to meet them. They shared a long road together, all the way back to when he was an actor championing the DPs. But going back even further, when their ancestors, people like B.E. Kertchman met people like Nellie Reagan and Pastor Ben Cleaver. The battle against Soviet Communism was present at the start and at the finish of Ronald Reagan's life, as was his kinship with the Jewish people.

It was in the 1970s that for the first time Christians started praying for the release of what they heard were "Prisoners of Zion" inside the Iron Curtain.

1950 Reagan and Nellie

In 1980, when Reagan entered the White House, he began his persistent pressure on the Soviets by echoing Moses' demand to "Let my people go!"

It was Reagan's constant pressure on Soviet leader Gorbachev that eventually led to the prying open of Soviet gates and releasing a million descendants of Abraham who immigrated into Israel in the early 90's.

The blessing to Israel and especially to the economy, science, medical, technology, education and all other aspects of Israeli life must be greatly credited to "the Gipper".

One of Reagan's favorite screen roles was that of a Notre Dame football player named George Gipp. His most memorable lines were as Gipp lay

dying and begged Coach Rockne to someday tell a future team that was facing a likely defeat the following, "I've got to go, Rock. It's all right. I'm not afraid. Some time, Rock, when the team is up against it, when things are wrong and the breaks are beating the boys, ask them to go in there with all they've got and win just one for the Gipper..."

I believe that our Heavenly Father has provided our nation with several

'Gippers' at key times in our nation's history over the years.

Those All-American 'Gippers', the presidents we are studying, made a difference for the Jewish people and the state of Israel. By being a blessing to Abraham's descendants, they brought a blessing on our nation.

These unlikely heroes came from the most diverse of backgrounds. They were poor boys and a rich boy, college graduates and one who never got beyond high school, a farmer, a rancher, a lawyer, a sports announcer, a real estate tycoon, two army officers, two naval officers and one military school cadet, two Democrats and three Republicans, one west coaster, one east coaster and three mid-westerners.

They were about as varied a group as you can find in this nation. But they all had one thing in common - they were in the right place at the right time with the intestinal fortitude to do what was right for the United States and for God's Chosen People.

George Gipp

When the time was right, they were ready to persevere against all the odds. And yes, they definitely won one for 'the Gipper'!

> **"You can tell a lot about a fellow's character by his way of eating jellybeans." Reagan**

When Ronald Reagan ran for Governor of California in 1966, he began eating "Goelitz Mini Jelly Beans" as part of his successful attempt to give up pipe smoking. An Oakland-based producer of the jelly beans sent a monthly shipment to the Governor's Office throughout Reagan's two terms in Sacramento. The company also made a custom-designed jelly bean jar for Reagan. After Reagan left the governorship, he continued to receive shipments directly from the company. Three and a half tons of red, white, and blue jelly beans were shipped to Washington, DC for the 1981 Inaugural festivities. The Herman Goelitz Candy Company provided the Reagan White House with jelly beans for all eight years of Reagan's presidency.

They received official Government authorization to develop a special jelly bean jar with the Presidential Seal on it. These Presidential jars, each in its own blue gift box, were given by Reagan to heads of state, diplomats, and many other White House guests. President Reagan's favorite flavor was licorice.

194

"To paraphrase Winston Churchill, I did not take the oath I have just taken with the intention of presiding over the dissolution of the world's strongest economy."

Reagan

"Government is like a baby. An alimentary canal with a big appetite at one end and no sense of responsibility at the other." Reagan

"Trust, but verify."
Reagan

Reagan and Trump Compared and the Jewish Vote

It is only in retrospect of three decades that some similarities and differences of the Reagan and Trump administrations are beginning to be compared. Still, it is way too early to properly assess the longer-term achievements of Donald Trump in relation to Israel and the Jewish people in comparison to Reagan's time in office.

Although the Reagan agenda was clearly more conservative than the views of the American Jewish community, over the course of his two terms, Jewish fears of Reagan bringing on Armageddon diminished. However, the American Jewish fear of a constitutional amendment for prayer in schools lingered on the back burner. Even on the issue of Israel, the American Jewish fear of Reagan proved to be unfounded. Although the 1982 Reagan Plan for Middle East peace was panned by both the Israeli government and American Jewish leaders, Reagan eventually came to be seen as one of the best friends Israel has had in the White House.

This evolution happened even though the original inner circle around Reagan had few relationships with the organized Jewish community. That is certainly not the case for Trump. His closest associates include Orthodox Jews (David Friedman is his ambassador to Israel) and his Sabbath-observing daughter and son-in-law.

As a Pro-Israel Christian Zionist, I am often asked by American Christians, **"Why do Jews vote like they do?"**
What they mean by that is they read that American Jews often vote for candidates who are not pro-Israel or on the side of anti-Torah issues as LGBTQ, abortion, anti-circumcision, physician-assisted death, etc.
"Why would Jews belong to a Democratic party that has excluded any reference to God or Jerusalem in their platform?" is another common question I hear.

Many Gentile Christians are astounded at the lack of support by the Jewish voters even for a candidate with seemingly excellent Israeli connections. There is a widely held assumption that American Jews have Israel at the top of their priority list when it comes to voting.

The truth is that the issue of Israel is seldom near the top of that list, nor has it been for at least three decades. Liberal democratic issues rank much higher on the American Jewish priority list than does the state or even the security of Israel.

Where, you may ask, is the American Jewish support for the state and people of Israel? If Israel is not that important, what does fire up Jewish Americans when it comes to election time? In short, the Jewish precept of *tikkun olam* ("repairing the world"), is interpreted by modern mainstream Jews to mean "social justice."

The Liberal definition of "social justice" fits nicely into the planks of the Democratic party platform.

When expanding the term "social" into "socialism" it suddenly sounds new, fresh and appealing, even though it has a one-hundred-year track record of failure in other nations.

When the term "liberal" became discredited because of the failure in practice of the liberal programs, the same politicians marched on under a new-old banner called "Progressivism."

Although that term was retired after its heyday and failure in the late 19th and early 20th centuries, it was taken out of the "Museum of Retired and Failed Political Ideas", dusted off and worn by Hillary Clinton like a suffragette sash for a week or two.

The trouble was "Progressive" just didn't sound like it was speeding forward or progressing fast enough in the Twitter age.

So, what does all of this inside politics have to do with Presidential candidates who support Israel anyway?

Election results over the past 60 years consistently show that the American Jewish vote will go to the most liberal candidate. They literally fear the conservative one, no matter their record or positions on Israel.

"US-Israel relations" was the most important issue for only 7.2% in the American Jewish Committee's study of Jewish American Opinion. US-Israel relations ranked fifth behind the "economy" (41.7%), "national security" (12.3%), "healthcare" (12%), and "income inequality" (11.6%).

Presuming that Israel is extremely important to them, millions of dollars have been wasted in an attempt to sway Jewish voters. Israel was the "most important" voting issue for a mere 4% of respondents in the Public Religion Research Institute's 2012 Jewish Values survey. Israel was one of two top "voting issue priorities" for just 10% in another poll conducted around the same time.

It is time to face the fact that Israel is no longer anywhere near the top issues that influence American Jewish voters. Recent studies consistently show that the American Jewish community and Israeli society exist in two very different realities and these differences have shaped and hardened their world views of each other.

As we move into the new Trump political era it is more important than ever for Israelis, American Jews and Christian Zionists to try to better understand each other. Learning about their priorities we then must treat each other and those beliefs with mutual respect.
There may well come a time when the combined American Jewish and Pro-Israel Christian communities will need to band together on that singular issue in upcoming elections... or not.

Trump meets Reagan 1987

198

RONALD REAGAN

DONALD TRUMP

-Mocked and not considered to be a serious candidate before winning the Presidency

- Was a TV celebrity before running for office

- Was a Democrat before switching to Republican

- Used "Make America Great Again" as his campaign slogan

-Attacked by a protester at the podium during a speech

- Used straight talk and humor to communicate with supporters

- Became the oldest President elected

- 1st President that had a divorce

-Suceeded a Democrat President

- Pro immigration but strongly against illegal immigration

-Pro life, Pro 2nd Ammendment, and Pro tax reduction

- Initialy considered to "not be a true conservative" by the Establishment but increased GOP voter turnout and became a Republican Party Icon and beloved President

-Mocked and not considered to be a serious candidate despite being the GOP frontrunner

- Was a TV celebrity before running for office

-Was a Democrat before switching to Republican

-Using "Make America Great Again" as his campaign slogan

-Attacked by a protester at the podium during a speech

- Uses straight talk and humor to communicate with supporters

-Would become the oldest President if elected

- Would be the 2nd President that had a divorce

-Would suceed a Democrat President

-Pro Immigration but strongly against illegal immigration

-Pro life, Pro 2nd Ammendment, and Pro tax reduction

-Considered to "not be a true conservative" by the establishment but has increased GOP voter turnout considerably from the last two elections and can potentially become a Republican Party Icon and beloved President

PART 5

DONALD JOHN
TRUMP

Donald John Trump (born June 14, 1946)

is the 45th and current president of the United States. Before entering politics, he was a businessman and television personality. Vice president Mike Pence. Trump was preceded by Barack Obama. He has unusual political affiliations: Republican (1987–1999, 2009–2011, 2012–present); Democratic (until 1987, 2001–2009) ,Reform (1999–2001) Independent (2011–2012).

INTRODUCTION

"I will bless those who bless you, and whoever curses you I will curse; and all peoples on earth will be blessed through you."
Genesis 12:3 (NIV)

God will bless those who bless Abraham's descendants (the Jews of today). God emphatically promised (that's to put the emphasis on it), that He would always bless those who blessed Abraham's descendants. But perhaps this promise of God has been 'over-used' by Christian Zionists? Those of us who love and attempt to be a blessing to the Jewish people use that verse so often that it may sound like a meaningless mantra to those who don't understand or comprehend it at the same level we think we do. I'm using the word 'mantra' purposely because it is defined as, "a sacred formula believed to possess magical power used in prayer and incantation."

If we off-handedly recite the Genesis 12:3 section to those who 'don't get it', doesn't it sound like some Buddhist Zen chanting of the ten names of Buddha over and over?

Certainly, we believe the Godly Covenant instituted into the world order (olam) when God first made it with Abram and his descendants forever. But to just rattle it off and not to honestly inquire of the listener, "Do you know what I'm talking about when I say, "Genesis 12:3" or "God will bless those who bless Abraham's descendants"?

Please consider taking the time to clarify what you are basing your actions and your words on. Remember, we are not just doing something for the Jews so we can get something back from God. We are doing it because it aligns our actions with a Godly principle that impels our actions to be based on belief in His Word.

Often, when looking back in time, we're bound to say, "Wow! God used the most unlikely and unqualified people to assist in carrying out His plans. They weren't qualified and even some of them weren't especially willing. What an amazing sense of humor, irony and surprise God has."

Yes, it's an amazing thing. The people that you and I would never have chosen, are often the ones God chooses and uses.
Why would He do that? Is it accidental?
Of course not. God does it on purpose so that you and I, who are just ordinary people, from the world's vantage point "nobodies" like you and me, should take heart and realize that God can and will use us, no matter how large or small our footprint is. Many folks are discouraged because they are not well known in the world. Most ministers will never manage to fill their churches, let alone pack stadiums and arenas.

However, God's Word and history shows that He carries out His plan. And that He can and will use anyone He wants to whatever their background or worldly credentials.

The media and the political experts are mystified when the 'unlikely and unqualified' (by worldly standards) are elevated to positions of national leadership.

The 'Accidental' Presidents

In the previous chapters we discussed men that could be labeled as 'accidental' presidents. By past political standards there was just no way they were ever going to be elected to the presidency of the United States.

One of them never attended college, not even for a single day. The only old picture we have of him shows his backside, while he is looking at the southside of a team of horses pulling a plow north. I imagine that as he was plowing that same Missouri field for the umpteenth time, he probably thought, "My life is going nowhere."

And yet, God had something in mind for **Harry Truman**. He didn't realize that when was about six- or seven-years old, a 'seed' had been planted in his life.

The pensive little fella with the cowboy hat sits on the porch of the tiny 'Dog Trot' ranch house where he was born on the bank of the Pedernales River near Stonewall, Texas.

Times were hard for his family living out in the Texas hill country as his father was often unable to make a living on the ranch. He was forced to take on all kinds of part-time jobs and eventually, the family had to leave the ranch in 1914. It was about this time that Granddad put the six-year-old **L.B. Johnson** on his knee and planted a 'seed' that would sprout when he entered the Oval Office. Only God knows why He had selected this little boy and put a burning desire in his heart. All his life, the longing smoldered in his heart and mind to someday become President of the United States.

Classmates recalled that at the age of twelve he was already announcing that one day he'd be the President. It was his life-long driving force. But, despite all his efforts he eventually had to conclude that it wasn't going to happen. And then it did!

Our third most unlikely to ever become president was a persistent overachiever who seemed doomed to fail. While at Whittier high school, he just 'had' to play football even though he was a remarkably poor athlete. He also 'had' to do a lot of other things that he wasn't good at. His personality tended to make him a loner and a thinker. He entered politics as a candidate and yet hated going out and mixing with crowds, which you must do even if you are only running for Dogcatcher.

In 1960, he relentlessly campaigned for the presidency only to lose a close race to handsome Jack Kennedy. Not wanting to abandon politics he returned home to California and again failed in his bid to be elected Governor of his own home state. That second embarrassing defeat within two years made him emphatically declare that he was through with politics for good. During his famous concession speech, he told the press that this was his last election campaign and that, "… they wouldn't have Dick Nixon to kick around anymore." At that depressing time in his life he may have faced (and momentarily believed) the fact that he could never have another chance to become president.

At times, he would tell the story about his stern Quaker mother telling her six or seven-year-old son that if he was, "…ever in a position of power and a situation arose in which the Jews needed help, you, Richard, must do so!" Apparently, that motherly directive was not lost on young Richard when in 1973 his secretary of State told him about a three AM phone call from the terrified Israeli Ambassador, who urgently relayed Premier Golda Meir's plea for help on the third day of the Yom Kippur War. He reasoned that this tearful Jewish mother's plea was what his mother had planted in his heart so many years before. Even though **Richard Nixon**'s presidency was circling down the drain in the Watergate Scandal, he was there at the right place and the right time (with just the right seed implanted in his memory) to help save the state of Israel.

The one exception to our rule of being selected as unqualified, unwilling and unprepared to be president seems to be **Ronald Reagan.** He arrived on the political scene with the bearing, the good looks and the calm reassuring personality which all added up to a close-to-perfect presidential candidate.

His long career in Hollywood had formed Reagan's public image into the ideal of a strong American male. His Hollywood roles inevitably cast him as a soft-spoken strong honest athlete/cowboy. Although his critics and political foes tried to paint him as an empty-headed actor, he debuted on the political scene just when the voters were sick and tired of traditional politicians. His ease and composure before crowds and on television allowed him to go over the heads of obstructionist politicians and connect directly with the American public.

The incumbent Jimmy Carter was easily defeated, and Reagan later won a landslide victory over Walter Mondale for his second term. Only in retrospect we realize what incredible things he did for the present state of Israel. His continued insistence to release the 'prisoners of Zion' ultimately caused the locked gates of the USSR to swing open so that over one and a half million Jews could leave.

Three decades later, that influx of Jews into the Promised Land has propelled Israel into the forefront of the high-tech and military armament industries.

Reagan may have done more for the economy of Israel than any of his predecessors. He also became the first American president to formally authorize the signing of a "Strategic Cooperation Agreement" between Israel and the US. Despite some strains and bumps in the road, relations between America and Israel were stronger at the end of Reagan's tenure than ever before.

So, now we're ready to introduce the next president in this book (start the drum roll)!

"Ladies and gentlemen! Get ready for the most unique, most combative, most loved and most despised of all the 43 men who had preceded him in office. In the center ring the world's greatest deal-maker, the man who never sleeps and the world's fastest and most devastating Tweeter, his majesty - **Donald John Trump!**"

TRUMP
MAKE AMERICA GREAT AGAIN!

Americans are hungry to feel once again a sense of mission and greatness.

RONALD REAGAN

"When you open your heart to patriotism, there is no room for prejudice. The Bible tells us, 'How good and pleasant it is when God's people live together in unity'." Trump

The "Trump Miracle"

Who would have imagined in the 1960's that a wild and wealthy out-of-control kid from Queens would one day be President. The son of a builder and developer in New York City celebrated his seventieth birthday without ever having been elected to even a school board.

Even when he mounted his presidential campaign, he was the worst of 17 other, much better qualified Republicans. Although he had no political experience ,it was amazing to see all the other candidates crash like bowling pins to the cannon ball express, street-fighting tactics of this uncouth political neophyte.

Then he had to go up against the most powerful political machine ever assembled, the unstoppable Clinton Colossus and all its enablers. The experts predicted it was going to be a bloodbath where the rich and brash New Yorker would be carried comatose (or worse) out of the ring. As we now know, it didn't exactly turn out that way. Donald launched one into the cheap seats by smashing the ultimate Grand Slam in his first trip to the plate. It was such an incredible, unlikely turn of events that many of us came to believe that God must have intervened and put him in the lineup.

However, the Lord didn't put him there to boost his ego (that was already pumped on steroids) but for a Godly reason. The more his embattled first years in office unfolded, it became readily apparent to those who have eyes to see and ears to hear, that the reason for his miraculous ascendancy in Washington has to do with his refreshing and unequaled relationship and support of Israel.

Had the Obama administration continued by electing his selected woman to become his heir, our relationship with Israel undoubtedly would have gone off the edge of the cliff. If that had happened it would have brought a curse on the United States.

> **"Hillary Clinton has perfected the politics of personal profit and theft. She ran the State Department like her own personal hedge fund - doing favors for oppressive regimes, and many others, in exchange for cash."** Trump

But... it seems that out of nowhere, we've gotten a president who certainly is - according to all the pundits - unlikely, unbelievably uncouth, unacceptable, unreasonable, unhinged and highly unqualified.

Never mind all the 'un-'s. The more there are, the clearer it becomes (at least for me) to see that he was put there by God for those very 'un-' reasons. Many stunned pundits called it the 'Trump Miracle'.
Experts were flabbergasted when the tide changed during the election night.

"Indeed: God chose the foolish things of the world to shame the wise; God chose the weak things of the world to shame the strong. God chose the lowly things of this world and the despised things—and the things that are not—to nullify the things that are, so that no one may boast before Him." 1 Corinthians 1: 27-29

"I have made the tough decisions, always with an eye toward the bottom line. Perhaps it's time America was run like a business." Trump

It was such a surprise, shock and shame to the expert opinion-makers when an obviously 'unelectable' had legitimately been elected to the White House. If Chester A. Reilly (of *The Life of Reilly* fame) had been prognosticating on election night he would have said with all the exasperation he could muster, "What a revoltin' development this is!"

> The "Life of Riley" is an American radio situation comedy series of the 1940s that was adapted into a 1949 feature film, a 1950s television series, and a 1958 comic book.

I think there is little doubt that Donald J. Trump has elbowed his way into the hierarchy of God's 'accidental' presidents as a God-inspired, "revoltin' development."

In previous chapters we have seen how each of the 'Accidentals' was seeded early in life with an event or a phrase implanted that bloomed later in life when they were in the presidential office.

Donald Trump's father had a Lutheran background while his mother's

family was Church of Scotland (Scottish equivalent of Presbyterian). The president hesitantly talked about his religious beliefs during his 2016 presidential campaign. He often stated that his own book, *The Art of the Deal,* was his second favorite book, after the Bible.

Some critics and even bemused supporters have cited his vague answers when asked about details on religious matters. Stories are often cited about him nearly putting cash in a Church communion plate and referring to the communal wine and bread as "my little wine" and "my little cracker". During a speech at Liberty University he said "Two Corinthians" instead of the more familiar "Second Corinthians".

When asked about his familiarity with Biblical texts he replied with typical 'Trumpesque', "That's how my mother always said it."

The Trump family definitely had a Biblical background.

> **"I have a Bible near my bed." Trump**

Trump's Early-life Training
which Cause him to be a Blessing to the Jews

Presidents Johnson and Nixon referred to an admonition that was fixed in them by a family adult (Nixon's mother and Johnson's grandfather and Aunt Jessie). Undoubtedly, young Donald had it implanted by his New York born German-American father, who had a life-long relationship with the Jews of New York as well as from his Scottish mother.

In the Outer Hebrides chain of islands on the western side of Scotland is an island called Lewis.

In 1912, a child was born in the village of Tong. It was the tenth and last child of fisherman Malcolm MacLeod and his wife, Mary Smith.
That poor little girl from the farthest reaches of the treacherous North Sea, often described as being "perched at the edge of the world", was destined to become the mother of the most unlikely candidate to ever become an American president.
But not just any American president - to this date he is the one that consistently has done more for Israel than any of the previous presidents.

14 year-old Marry Anne

In 1930, eighteen year old Mary Anne MacLeod left her tiny ancestral island of Lewis for the wilds of New York, US of A. She was leaving behind a large extended family which included two elderly aunts who are credited with birthing something very special and unique in the mid-20th century.

In the late 1940's those two octogenarian sisters, Peggy and Christine Smith, were living in a small cottage in the village of Barvas on Lewis island. Blind Peggy and crippled Christine were homebound. Unable to attend public worship, their humble cottage became a Prayer War Room where they were constantly pleading with God for a true revival for their Hebrides Island homeland. For years, those elderly ladies continually asked God to move in their small Scottish fishing village and in the surrounding islands.

Day and night, they pleaded the Biblical promise: "I will pour water upon him that is thirsty and floods upon the dry ground." (Isaiah 44:3) After receiving a vision that the empty churches would be filled to overflowing with youth and a strange preacher in the pulpit, these two Gaelic-speaking sisters persuaded their local pastor to gather his elders and join in earnest prayer for revival. This continued for about six weeks and then one of the sisters insisted that their pastor bring the man she had seen in the vision to their pulpit. After three invitations "that man in the pulpit," the Scottish Reverend Duncan Campbell, landed on Lewis Island and the rest is history.

Rev. Duncan Campbell and the Lewis sisters

The following years were described by a resident as, "...a mighty outpouring of God's Spirit which occurred throughout the island in a three-year period from 1949-1952."
The Smith sisters' prayers and their persuasive insistence to invite Duncan Campbell to their village initiated a world-famous, miraculous revival and undeniable movement of God.

After the Smith sisters niece, Mary Anne MacLeod, emigrated to New York, she met a young carpenter whom she married. His name was Fred Christian Trump. Mary Anne and Fred had several children including a wild-haired blonde son most likely named after her cousin, Donald Smith (one of the first converts in the revival).

The Trump siblings — from left, Robert, Elizabeth, Freddy, Donald and Maryanne — in an undated photo. (Photo courtesy of the Trump family).
Donald is the fourth child of Fred and Mary Trump's five children. Maryanne Trump Barry, Donald's eldest sister, is a senior judge on the U.S. Court of Appeals for the 3rd Circuit. His older brother, Fred Jr., was a gregarious airline pilot but suffered from alcoholism and died at the age of 43. Donald often cites Fred Jr.'s death as a reason that he abstains from alcohol and cigarettes. Elizabeth Grau the third Trump child was an administrative secretary, and Trump's younger brother, Robert, went into business.

I wonder whatever became of that boy...

We do know that Mary returned to her home on Lewis Island practically every year and was certainly familiar with the revival of 1949-1953. Wouldn't it be interesting to know what Donald's mother told him about the Hebrides Revival?

I am certain that in 1946, Mary Anne's aunts prayed for their niece's latest baby boy who was named Donald. Isn't it wonderful to know that you are never too old or too infirm to impact the future generations by your prayers?

Only God knows what effect those prayers emanating from that Scottish cottage in the 1940s had on the presidency of the United States in 2016 and beyond.

Presidential visit to his mother's childhood home on Lewis Island. Ri. Mary Anne

More Childhood Influences

There is another spiritual side to this Trumpian mystery of the childhood influences that planted and tended the 'Jewish seeds' in this future president's life.

It started in the former European region of Galicia, an ancient name for a landlocked area between Poland and the Ukraine. Following World War I, Galicia had been taken over by the Soviets and became subsumed into the Ukraine. Even under Soviet occupation, many inhabitants of the former Galician cities remained secretly aligned with the Germans. This pro-German faction was overjoyed when the Nazi forces of the Fuehrer invaded in 1941.

Naturally, they were very much aligned with the anti-Semitism of the invaders as they drove the Russians to the east and often participated in the Jewish slaughters that followed.

In the early 1940s two Polish cities with large Jewish populations each had well-known Rabbis. In the town of Belz the 18-year-old son of the rabbi, Yisrael Wagner was betrothed to the daughter of the esteemed rabbi of the town of Buczacz (*Boo-Cahtch*).
Her name was Esther ('Rivka') Willig.
Rivka was described by a

Buczacz before the war

family member as the headstrong, charming and somewhat spoiled 'Rabbi's daughter' who often accompanied her elderly and universally beloved father on his appointments and duties. Quite naturally she was treated as a princess by his congregants.

In Jewish law, marriage consists of two separate ceremonies, the first of which is the betrothal which formally defines the engagement. There is a legal religious document committing both families to the future marriage of the young couple. The actual marriage ceremony was to be held at a later to be determined date, upon which the marriage was to be consummated.

However, before the wedding took place both towns were invaded by the German Nazi forces. Rivka's father was forced to provide the invaders with the names of the Jews in Buczacz. When word reached the elderly rabbi that all the young men on the list were subsequently rounded up and murdered just outside the town it had a devastating effect on the old, gentle man. He died of a stroke, brought on by remorse and feelings of guilt for the information he had unwittingly given to the SS murderers.

215

The Holocaust in occupied Poland
Extermination camp
Main city with ghetto
Major concentration camp

Before World War II, approximately 10,000 Jews (half of the local population) lived in Buczacz. About 7,000 Jews from that town were killed during the Nazi occupation.

Rivka and her mother went into hiding, but their hiding place was pointed out to the SS and they were thrown onto a train headed to the Belzec extermination camp.

Before locking them in a cattle car with more than 200 other Jews, the Nazis told them they were being taken out of the war zone for their protection.

Rivka didn't believe that lie for a moment.

As the train slowly chugged towards its deathly destination, Rivka begged her mother to allow her to jump from the train's tiny upper window. "No!" her mother responded.

For several hours Rivka pleaded and begged for her mother's blessing to escape. Finally, the strong-willed daughter prevailed. With her mother's blessing, people helped her push a water barrel towards the window.

Carefully, Rivka removed the slats and barbed wire and after one last look at her mother's tear-stained and care-worn face, she slithered out of the narrow window.

Rivka jumped and rolled off the embankment into a cornfield where Nazi gunfire from the top of the train whistled past. There in the corn rows, the train continued its way. Suddenly Rivka realized that she had no idea where she was, where to go or whom she could trust. It was then that she heard footsteps in the corn row and unintelligible voices. After a terrifying moment she heard men talking in Yiddish. The young men, who had also jumped from the train, were not hurt by the firing Nazi guards. They argued with her when she told them she had to return to Buczacz and find the hiding place where she had secreted an important false document that identified her as Polish Catholic Gentile and not Jewish.

Rivka managed to sneak back into town and reach the hiding place. Unbeknownst to anyone, she had pawned her engagement ring and from the money paid for the forged document.

The papers enabled her to travel to the capital city of Warsaw where she hid under various disguises, such as a Polish-Catholic domestic servant at the home of non-Jewish Polish families. Each time she was exposed as a Jew, Rivka miraculously escaped. Then one day, a German anti-aircraft unit retreating back into Germany commandeered the "Gentile-Polish" cook. Strangely enough, she ended the war as a Polish cook in a German military unit. God was certainly watching over "Paula," her Polish pseudonym, and helped her miraculously escape detection again and again for nearly four and a half years.

1943 Paulina Velanska a.k.a. Rivka Willig

Ironically, after Germany's surrender Rivka had a difficult time attempting to prove to the authorities that she was really Jewish and not a Polish collaborator cooking for the Nazis. Finally, after pleading her case to a US Army Rabbi, she was quickly admitted into a camp for Jewish survivors.

At the war's end in May 1945, destroyed Central Europe was filled with countless Jewish survivors wandering and searching for any surviving family members or former acquaintances. Rivka found shelter in a Displaced Persons (DP) Camp where she began teaching the children. Still, her heart was fixed on finding out the fate of her fiancée Yisrael.

It had been more than four years since she had seen or heard from him and she couldn't go on with her life until she had closure about the fate of her betrothed.

Rivka informed the Camp rabbi that she needed to return to her hometown of Buczacz to search for evidence or witnesses as to the fate of Yisrael. The camp rabbi tried everything he could think of to dissuade her from going back to Buczacz because there were rumors (later proved to be accurate) that Jews were being murdered in the streets of their hometowns in Poland and the Ukraine by civilians who had taken possession of their homes when the Jews were taken away. But Rivka was insistent and determined to go and get some answers and hopefully get married and have a family. Her mind was made up and she was going to leave on Sunday, after the Shabbat.

DP Camp Bergen-Belsen

That Friday afternoon, a young man entered the office of that same rabbi, asking for help with a problem. The rabbi told him to come back on Sunday, after the Shabbat, and he would talk to him then.

Seeing the distraught look on the young man's face, the rabbi said, "Okay, walk with me on my way and tell me your problem and after Shabbat we'll see what we can do."

The young man responded with a typical story such as the rabbi had heard so many times before. He was unable to find a loved one and he had exhausted all his resources, etc. etc.

"Alright, tell me her name and where she lived before the war."

"Well Rabbi, her first name is Esther and she was from Buczacz in the Ukraine. If she is alive she'd be almost 21 now."

The rabbi was stunned by the answer, but there would certainly be more than one 'Esther' among the 10,000 Jews from Buczacz. "Did she have a nickname and what was her family name?"

The young man, whose name was Yisrael, said, "We called her Rivka and her last name was Willig."

Not wishing to raise false hopes, the rabbi weighed the evidence. Finally, he told the young man, "You can stop searching."

To Yisrael, who had followed so many false leads only to find nothing, the answer could only mean that there was proof of her death and the search should be called off. Seeing the crestfallen look on Yisrael's face, the rabbi hastened to say, "*Baruch HaShem*! She's alive! She's here in the camp! Your Rivka lives!"

Soon thereafter Rivka and Yisrael married in Salzburg, Austria and together embarked on a long trip that took them to Bolivia, California and eventually Brooklyn, New York.

Yisrael continued his long-interrupted studies and was rabbinically ordained. The young rebbe and his rebbetzin were appointed to a neighborhood in Brooklyn named Beach Haven. In the baby boom years following world War II, there was a great need for housing and new high -rise apartments were springing up in the area. Some of them were mostly inhabited by Jewish refugee tenants. Rabbi Wagner was warned that most of those Jews weren't religious and there wasn't much likelihood that a permanent synagogue could be established. But since he was new, he could use the parking garage under the apartment building.

Rabbi Wagner's son, himself a rabbi in Israel today, added the following to the narrative,

"As soon as it was established, this shul quickly had a minyan of European Jews who wanted to pray together. It began with thirty members but rapidly grew to one hundred families. My father exuded warmth and friendliness and they loved the experience of the shul, my father's heartfelt manner and his Chassidic ways."

Because of the rapid growth of the congregation, it soon became apparent that the parking garage was inadequate and inappropriate for a house of worship. They were hesitant to ask the owner and landlord of the building because he was a well-known German-American (who often pretended that he was Swedish, which didn't fool any of the Jewish Europeans who were survivors of Hitler's German-Nazi fanaticism and genocide).

Reasoning that this was America after all, the rabbi was only going to ask for a room to come together. Besides, his congregation, including himself, were this man's tenants. The rabbi was not in the least intimidated when he learned that the German landlord also owned at least 31 other apartments in the neighborhood. What if he was turned down or insulted when he approached the owner? That kind of slight could never compare with what he had endured during the war. After all, with his faith in God, Who had helped him to survive those four war years, it didn't seem so daunting to approach that German building owner.

The rabbi's son continued the story,

"My father had an idea," recalled HaRav Wagner. "Although he did not know the owner personally, even though he was his landlord, but he felt that if he explained to him that his tenants, the vast majority of whom were Jewish refugees, needed a synagogue nearby, it would mean something special to him. He also sensed that he was possibly a religious man, and this might appeal to him."

"My father approached him from a business angle as well as with an emotional appeal. They both knew that a community centered around a synagogue would radiate spiritual energy and its members would be decent, upright people. The owner would also benefit financially from such a population who would be good tenants."

This first meeting laid the foundation for a relationship that blossomed into a 48 year friendship between Fred and the rabbi and their wives. Upon hearing about the situation, not only did the German owner donate land for the synagogue, but he also gave a large donation towards the construction of an imposing building that became known as the Beach Haven Jewish Center.

"Fred even attended the cornerstone laying. They met over and over again. Fred saw my father as a holy person and a very wise man. He used to call him, 'My rabbi' and Fred often ended their conversations by theologically reminding Rabbi Yisrael, 'Remember, rabbi, you and I both worship the same God.'"

"For years, Fred and my father met throughout the year, but officially as well - once a year, when Fred would ceremoniously donate a sizable sum for the shul. In reality, most of the money the shul needed came from Fred." Rabbi Wagner said that those generous donations swelled in size over the years.

"Occasionally my Father told Fred about various needy Jewish families living in the neighborhood. Fred always came through with generous sums for them."

The German landlord's first and middle names were Frederick and Christ - not names that would endear him to a Jewish Orthodox rabbi. It seemed everyone just called him 'Fred'.

Did I forget to mention that Fred's last name was **TRUMP?**
That's right! You read it correctly. It was Frederick Christ TRUMP (1905-1999), the father of Donald J. Trump, the 45th President of the United States.

FRED C. TRUMP, who donated the land for the Talmud Torah of the Beach Haven Jewish Center, 723 Ave. Z, discusses the impressive future with the assemblage at last week's ground-breaking.

Often, Donald J. Trump recalled how he followed his father around construction sites. Undoubtedly, he was present at some of the meetings his father had with his rabbi friend. He certainly witnessed the respect and affection they had for each other.

Both Rav Wagner Jr. and his sister Malky often saw Donald on a weekly basis in the laundry room of their apartment building.
Malky, who lives in Israel and works at Yad VaShem recalled,

"I remember Donald from the age of about 14 or 15, with his wild shock of blond hair and his endless reserves of energy and drive. His father used to send him to collect the money from the laundry machines. Fred taught his children from a very early age to take responsibility; he gave them no breaks. Donald may have been wild as a youth, but his father raised him well."

Malki Weisberg, 4th child of Esther and Yisrael; Young Trump family; Donald left.

"I grew up in New York City, a town with different races, religions, and peoples. It breeds tolerance."
Trump

Hearing those words, I began to understand the early childhood training that Donald received. In terms of his stunning victory in the 2016 presidential elections, Rabbi Wagner Jr. has no doubt as to the reason: *"Donald's father had the zechus of paying for the new synagogue and maintaining it for years. Fred gave money to many struggling Jewish families and he gave great honor to the rav of the shul and to Jews in general. Donald thus has zechus avos, (God-given honor for his father's good deeds) and that, I believe, is what has brought him to the White House."*

> Zechus Avos means that one derives the merit of the good deeds of his parents or ancestors that brought him or assisted in bringing him good fortune, either financial or sources of pride and happiness in his family or the prominent position he himself might have obtained)

The one foreign leader that appears to have a lot in common with Donald Trump and has been a longtime acquaintance is Benjamin Netanyahu, the veteran Israeli Prime Minister.

It is interesting to note that after the second Israeli national election in 2019, when the outcome was again in question without a clear winner, President Trump was asked if he had phoned Netanyahu and discussed the as yet unknown election results.

Trump responded with an unexpected answer to a reporter's question. He implied that he did not call, and he said that, "Our national relationship is with the state of Israel."

Trump also pointed out the obvious, "The results are very close, and the next Prime Minister may not be determined until there is a further election."

Having been in Israel during that election, there was no hiding the fact that Netanyahu emphasized his closeness with Trump with billboards and building-sized photos of the two. As usual, the anti-Trump press turned his answer into a negative about his 'friendship' with the Israeli Premier. Trump was accused of not wanting anything to do with a 'loser' who couldn't clearly win two or even three elections in a row.

To examine the national relationship between Israel and the United States, it is instructive to look at one of Bibi's best-known statements about the bottom line on the Jewish state.

"What is the root of the conflict? ... the simple truth is that the root of the conflict was, and remains, the refusal to recognize the right of the Jewish people to a state of their own in their historic homeland."
Bibi, June 2009 Foreign Policy Speech Bar Ilan University

I know what you're thinking! Whenever closely examining and dissecting statements by politicians, you've discovered that there is nothing in them but a lot of fuzzy hot air with more caveats than a basket of worms. However, this time the words from this master politician are quite different – they actually have meat on their bones, and the content is packed with spiritual truth.

"What is the root of the conflict?" Netanyahu asked and then answered at the start of his second term as Prime Minister.

"Why are the Israelis and Palestinians in this seemingly endless fight that has no discernible end to it? What is the root of this battle? [What's it all about Alfie?]"
Netanyahu continued, **"The simple truth is that the root of the conflict was, is, and remains: the refusal to recognize the right of the JEWISH PEOPLE to a state of their own in their historic homeland."**

225

Translated into evangelical Christian lingo:
The Jewish people are God's Chosen People.

Dissecting Netanyahu's simple statement, we see the following:
1.   It is the refusal of the world powers, and especially the Palestinians, to recognize the existence of God having a Chosen People along with the God-given rights that belong to them.
2.   It is the refusal of the Palestinians and the United Nations to recognize the covenant of a God-given land-grant for that infinitesimally tiny slice of the planet.
"The right of the Jewish people to a state
of their own in their historic homeland."

Wat is their 'Historic Homeland'?

In 'Bible talk': that tiny piece of the globe is called "the Promised Land". Conclusion: all this conflict over Israel is because the world refuses to recognize that God still has a Chosen People and God still has a Promised Land!   And that, Alfie, in the proverbial nutshell, is what it's all about. The world, not just the Palestinians, refuses to even contemplate that a God exists who could have a plan that includes a national people like the dreaded Jews and a piece of land that covenantally would be preserved for their homeland. It is just too much for the world to acknowledge!

The world gladly uses the so-called 'Palestinians' as their stalking horse so they don't have to reveal their true hatred of the whole idea. In short: it all starts with a refusal to acknowledge the existence of a God and a Godly plan for the world and especially for the Chosen Jewish people and the Land that God promised to those same returnees. Undoubtedly you are thinking that I have been beating that same dead horse over and over.   Truthfully, I've never beaten a horse, but sometimes you really need to get their attention by a little controlled repetition.

Did I just hear you say, "OKAY, you made your point. I got it! "
Phew! That wasn't so hard, was it?

226

Isaiah (11:11) prophesied about this return of the Chosen People to the Promised Land when he wrote,
"In that day the Lord will reach out His hand a second time to reclaim the surviving remnant of His people."
The prophet Amos also referred to this present time when he stated,
"I will plant Israel in their own land, never again to be uprooted from the land I have given them."

We are now living in a time when God's Chosen People are coming back into that Promised Land. That is the reason why it is blooming agriculturally, financially, technologically and in countless other ways. The people of Israel are there to stay and they and the land will not be dismembered!

Upon hearing Netanyahu's succinct statement in 2009, this could possibly have been the reaction of the following people:

John Kerry looks is as if he is saying, "Oyoyoy! Who can believe this kind of stuff?"
Hillary Clinton would have gotten a big laugh out of it. "This is deplorable! Can anybody believe someone would say that?" she screams.
The idea that a politician could say something so far out as, "God has a chosen people and God has a promised land," would also have tickled **Obama.**
But you know what? It doesn't make President **Trump** laugh.

As a matter of fact, we have not seen a president who was so significantly focused on Israel and who worked so consistently to get

David Friedman

things done there. His son-in-law is involved, he has his own team focused on Israel and the new ambassador, David Friedman certainly brings a new ideological way of dealing with the same old problems.

All of them are definitely going about it in a new and exciting way.

An Unusual but Refreshing First Lady

God gave our president Trump a stalwart wife. Not only is she attractive (most people, except her enemies, will agree with that) but spiritually there is something special about her. In February of 2017, less than a month after entering the White House, the presidential couple flew to Melbourne, Florida for a political 'Thank You' rally. People had been waiting in and around a large hangar for hours for the president and the First Lady to arrive. As with most political rallies, upon their arrival there was all kinds of cheerleading, whistling and stomping going on.

People made a lot of noise; many wore silly hats and appeared to be having lots of fun. This crowd was really hyped up to see President Trump come back to Florida, the state that helped him win the election.

So, what happened next?
Instead of the president walking out on the stage, out came a cool and serene Melania. Her appearance ignited the crowd even more and they increased their shouting and applause. What Melania did next stunned them into silence. Gazing intently at the audience, she said, "Let us pray!"

Who ever heard of a modern rah-rah political rally starting with prayer? I thought, "Oh no, is this going to be one of those politically correct nothingness prayers occasionally muttered at ceremonies that have prayers as part of the protocol?"

But it was so touching to hear Melania's beautiful Slovenian accent leading the formerly rambunctious crowd in the Lord's Prayer and especially when she intoned, "and leeeed us not into temptation," and "deeeliver us from eeevil."

Reprieve and one More Chance

Of course, the press of the "Always hate everything Trumpers" and the "Never Trumpers" bloc derided her for daring to pray publicly.

But to those who truly believe in the power of prayer and the miracle we saw taking place on that stage - well, were thrilled. That moment made a grizzled old Marine unashamedly shed some tears and then a few more when a picture showed up of the president stoppingin midstride to bow his head in what looked like prayer.

That special moment, so different from anything else I've ever seen on a political stage, solidified the impression that entered my mind when I first heard the results of the 2016 election, "The Righteous Judge of the Universe has given our nation a **REPRIEVE!**"

He gave us one more chance because a reprieve is not a pardon! He gave us a reprieve from what we deserve because of all the things we have been approving which definitely are contrary to God's Word.

Our continued 'good behavior' can keep our country from the national destruction that other empires brought on themselves by cursing God, Israel and the Jewish people.

"People are so shocked when they find... out I am Protestant. I am Presbyterian. And I go to church, and I love God, and I love my church." Trump

---

The question remains unanswered as to how long the reprieve will remain in effect. Will we violate the terms and return to the Obama-Hillary-Kerry days of cursing our friends and blessing our enemies?

Prior to the 2016 election, a variety of ungodly laws had been instituted. Yet, suddenly, there was a sea change in the way the ship of state was sailing. To use another analogy… a new gun-slinging sheriff just galloped down Main Street …with a wife in the buckboard heading to the prayer meeting at the Longbranch.

As the Commander-in-Chief shook his head in disbelief, he said with an approving smile, "I didn't tell her to do that!" It was almost as if the president was wondering, *Where did that come from?*

The 'Trump Derangement Syndrome' victims immediately jumped on their twitters and railed that she had just brazenly violated the Constitutional statement of "the separation of Church and State" by publicly making people pray with her.

Of course, that phrase of "Church and State" is found nowhere in the Constitution. Besides, she is not a government official and even presidents have publicly prayed since the founding of our nation.

I have no doubt that Melania's prayer came from a heart that is sensitive to God's prodding and direction.

Trump opens first full day on job with a traditional church service

230

Which reminds me of a Biblical story. (I can hear my wife thinking, "What doesn't?")

I think (and hope) that there may be a parallel between what is going on here and the story that God gave us in the Bible. By the way, God didn't make up stories to put in there just to fill up the book and to make it look thicker (like I'm tempted to do).

Because everything in the Bible is there for our learning, let's see what we can learn about Presidents and Kings. If you are about to doze off and your eyelids are getting heavy, put the book down and do a couple of hundred **jumping-jacks** to get the blood flowing.
Ready?

As I'm going to take you into the book of Kings, all you have to remember are two names: Asa and Jehoshaphat. Father Asa and his son Jehoshaphat were both kings of Judah. Similar events happened in their lives but each reacted differently. The son (Jehoshaphat) made the right choice while his father (Asa) made the wrong choice.

Did the son learn from his father's mistake? How much did Donald learn from Fred? Their business lives were intertwined for many years just as the kingships of Asa and Jehoshaphat were undoubtedly intertwined.

OK, you can stop jumping now. Sit down and try to stay awake.

Let us take a look at 2 Chronicles 17:2

"Jehoshaphat placed troops in all the fortified cities of Judah and set garrisons in the land of Judah and in the cities of Ephraim which his father Asa had captured."

Jehoshaphat came to the throne of Judah when the nation was just about to go over the edge of the cliff.
Much like Trump when he entered office, Jehoshaphat was thrown into something that seemed like it was way over his head. The army was in very bad shape.

Doesn't that look similar to what was happening in our own country? During the previous eight years of Obama's administration our military had been hollowed out. The sequestered budget resulted in unbelievably large cuts to our military preparedness. These were supposed to be split evenly (by dollar amounts, not by percentages) between the defense and non-defense categories.

> That procedural guillotine was only meant to hang over the heads of the budget negotiators and to get them to compromise and come to a logical budget-cutting agreement. Sequestration was thought to be so outrageously crazy that it would be seen as such an intensely misguided, ill-considered, and poorly targeted method to achieve deficit reduction that it was assumed that the congressional negotiators would compromise long before resorting to it. Unfortunately, a compromise was not reached, and the "sequester" took effect.

Massive defense cuts piled up over the years of the Obama administration just like they did during the reign of Asa, the father of Jehoshaphat. We are in the process of rebuilding those military deficits. However, the years of sequestration cannot be fixed overnight. The Defense cuts averaged about 9% annually. The impact on troop levels, research and development and acquisition of new weapon systems and technology will be a long time coming back and be incredibly more expensive to rebuild.

> "Our military has to be strengthened. Our vets have to be taken care of. We have to end Obamacare, and we have to make our country great again, and I will do that." Trump

The first priority of a national leader is to protect his people, which calls for a robust military ready and able to defend the borders against intrusion and attack. Therefore, the first steps Jehoshaphat took were to strengthen his defenses. A major part of strengthening Judah's defenses was to build fortifications, especially on the border with the northern kingdom of Israel. He was fortifying his country. Doesn't that sound familiar? A king didn't have to be concerned about a House or Senate that might oppose his plans. The king didn't have to be concerned about being re-elected. He just had to guard against assassination and not the dreaded impeachment or a nasty media. As Mel Brooks would tell you, with a giant wink and smile, "It's good to be the king."

Many people voted for Trump because he promised, *"I am going to build a wall and the other guys are going to pay for it."* Everybody remembered that line in his stump speech and many people voted for him because of it.

When you look back on the last year in America under the leadership of President Donald Trump, there's only one way to describe it: **promises made, promises kept**.

— *Vice President Mike Pence*

That is exactly what Jehoshaphat did when he first came into his kingship. In his third year, Jehoshaphat established a rare innovation in his kingdom: a traveling school and faculty that was open to the public.

This mobile school, staffed by 16 well trained men, toured the Kingdom of Judah while teaching the laws of the LORD to the population. The initial idea was that the people would go up to Jerusalem and learn there, but Jehoshaphat said, "Go out and teach the Law of the Lord to the population. We have to get back to a Godly spiritual foundation in this country." It was rumored that the children began calling it a Torah-mobile when they heard the tinkling bells as it came down the road.

Trump attempted to free religious institutions from the fear of the dreaded Johnson Amendment. In 1954 Senator Lyndon Johnson included an amendment in a giant spending bill which drew no attention at the time. It was designed to shut down the opposition he was getting in his re-election bid from a couple of 501 (C) (3) non-profits from speaking or publishing against him in Texas. It wasn't until some years later that the ACLU and other left-wing advocacy groups figured out that they could keep churches (which are overwhelmingly tax exempt 501 (C) (3) organizations) from speaking out about political issues and candidates. The prohibition became part of the Internal Revenue code and to undo it will take an act of Congress.

Thus far, Trump has issued an Executive Order that instructs the IRS to ignore the amendment, but it is still on the books. It was hardly ever (if ever) used against a church to revoke its exemption. But, it did its damage as most pastors have been scared into silence when it comes to 'anything political'.

2 Chronicles 17:7-9
"In the third year of his reign he sent his officials... to teach in the towns of Judah.... Levites... and the priests... They taught throughout Judah, taking with them the Book of the Law of the LORD; [the Torah] they went around to all the towns of Judah and taught the people."

Not only was the country being defended but it was also strengthened spiritually. This was followed with an educational reform movement.

In our country, something similar began to happen with the appointment of **Betsy DeVos** as the Secretary of Education. She is devoted to reforming many of the failing school systems that have become a national disgrace. Because of her outspoken Christian positions and not having been part of the public education system, the well-funded and entrenched public-school teacher's union and the Democratic political party oppose her at each turn of the way.

I can't help but think that Jehoshaphat must have faced similar opposition to all the reforms he knew had to be made in order to fulfill his theme of "Making the Kingdom of Judah Great Again." Of course, Satan would have opposed the changes the king desired.

Thankfully, in our nation's history we have also had leaders who were not hesitant about bulling their way through the china shop and breaking a few teacups on the way, just like Jehoshaphat did.

Vs. 10: "The fear of the LORD fell on all the kingdoms of the lands surrounding Judah, so that they did not go to war against Jehoshaphat."

The nearby enemies of Judah realized something revolutionary was going on in Judah, so they pulled back and didn't attack the weakened kingdom as they had planned.

In the three years of the new sheriff's term, there has been a remarkable turnaround in the morale and discipline of the US military and a change in the rhetoric and actions of the North Korean dictator who had been rattling his nuclear missiles at the world. But we'll get back to that in a minute (if you're a fast reader).

Continuing to read the Jehoshaphat Chronicles in verse 11, we see that economics entered the revival.

11. "Some Philistines brought Jehoshaphat gifts and silver as tribute. "

That foreign tribute was an economic decision on their part. They concluded that just paying tribute as the losing enemy country would not have been enough to assure their survivability. Therefore, they wanted to buy a little extra protection from their other enemies. The ancient enemies of the Jews (the Philistines) not only willingly were bringing their imposed taxes, but also valuable presents.

Isn't it amazing what a strong leader inspires when the nation's priorities such as defense, education and spirituality are all in place?

In the US, the fair amount of taxable income on imported items as well as domestic taxes started to flow into the coffers because those taxpayers realized that it was being used properly and their daily way of life had vastly improved under honest leadership. When citizens are well informed and again have confidence in the wisdom and honesty of their leaders and the decisions they make, the citizen's trust level increases and the revenue flow into the government coffers increases and consequently an honest government is enabled to do more.

> **"We must speak our minds openly, debate our disagreements honestly, but always pursue solidarity."**
>
> **Trump**

Even *"the Arabs brought him flocks: seven thousand seven hundred rams and seven thousand seven hundred goats."*

It was amazing how the money started coming in to upgrade the nation. Of course, the Scriptures do not say or imply it, but a similar increase in revenues to our government occurred when tax cuts were initiated during the Reagan and Trump administrations. Did something like that occur in ancient Judea? Perhaps there was a reassessment of the tribute required from the Philistines and the Arabians because it seems to imply that there was a resurgence in their cooperation. Why would the ancient enemies of the Jews suddenly start bringing gifts and willingly pay their assigned taxes?

Was it not because they realized that they were really vassal-like states, not only in subjection to but also under the protection of Judah that was growing stronger by the day? It would be in their best interest to be on the best of terms with that kingdom.

Whenever possible, tribes and nations will logically conduct their affairs in their own best interests.

When you carefully read 2 Chronicles 17 verse by verse, it sounds very much like the times we are living in right now.

> *"12. Jehoshaphat became more and more powerful; he built forts and store cities in Judah 13. and had large supplies in the towns of Judah. He also kept experienced fighting men in Jerusalem."*
> Note that he didn't weaken his military because of sequestration; Judah's improving strength was fed by an increase in funds willingly paid, even by former enemies.
> *"14. Their enrollment by families was as follows...19 These were the men [read the names God put in there for a purpose] who served the king, besides those he stationed in the fortified cities throughout Judah."*

So, the military was rebuilt, the economy revived, and riches and honor were properly accorded to the king who had turned it all around. It seems that the ship of state should have had smooth sailing ahead. But the beauty of the Holy Scriptures is that it also highlights the warts and pimples of its heroes, only to remind us that they aren't saintly statues without human faults.

How does a king react to a just comeuppance from an advisor? History reveals that too often powerful leaders surround themselves with 'yes men' and shield themselves from criticism. When they become powerful and rich they are transformed into unreasonable people.

Keeping this in mind, look at the examples of his forefathers by going back in time.

"I try to learn from the past, but I plan for the future by focusing exclusively on the present. That's where the fun is."

Do you remember what Jehoshaphat's father Asa did in 2 Chronicles 16?

When his kingdom of Judah was threatened by the adjoining northern kingdom (Israel) Asa did not turn to God or to godly advisors for strategy, but instead applied *"The enemy of my enemy is my friend"* strategy as espoused centuries later by Sun Tzu.

> **Sun Tzu** was a Chinese general, military strategist, writer and philosopher who lived in the Eastern Zhou period of ancient China. Sun Tzu is traditionally credited as the author of *The Art of War,* an influential work of military strategy that has affected Western and East Asian philosophy and military thinking.

In the short term it may have looked like it was clever, but that wasn't how God would have directed the course of action. Much earlier in his reign (2 Chronicles 14) Asa had started off extremely well by cleansing the nation from idolatry, and God gave him a decade of peace to carry out the remainder of the work. He strengthened his cities and built walls (now there's a novel idea. I wonder if that idea ever occurred to Trump?).

"He sought the Lord and was given rest on every side, and so they built, and the economy of Judah prospered (14:7)."

Then Asa was confronted by an army coming up out of Egypt that appeared to be much larger and stronger than Judah's. The options of suing for peace or paying for pagan reinforcements must have occurred to young King Asa.

This likely was his first war. He was not a combat veteran like his forefather David had been. What did he do in the face of this vast existential threat? His prayer mimicked that of young David who spiritually recognized that Goliath and the Philistines were not challenging just another army but were going against the very *"God of the armies of Israel, whom you are defying."* (1 Sam. 17:45)

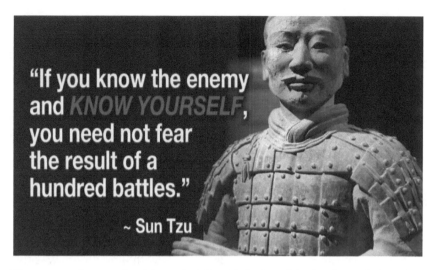

"If you know the enemy and *KNOW YOURSELF*, you need not fear the result of a hundred battles."

~ Sun Tzu

The reason for emphasizing what David declared in the face of the giant is to inspire us today. Like that ancient silent army of Israel that was cowed by one big NBA-like player and an early Johnson-like Amendment that had silenced an entire Jewish army. Something that had never happened before or since in history.

David's positive confession (some would say, "his twitter boasting ") was... *"so that the whole world will know that there is a God in Israel!"* (17:46-47) and not only that, but the truth is *"the Lord saves not with sword or spear! But better than that...the battle is the Lord's!"*

It was a miraculous outcome on the battlefield and the action was described as, *"The Lord struck down the Cushites before Asa and his men."* (2 Chron. 14:12). As a result of Asa turning to the Lord for help, not only did they decisively triumph on the field of battle but were rewarded with uncountable plunder, land, sheep and cattle. The kingdom and King Asa were greatly enriched. For a long period of time Asa was at rest from attack by his enemies.

> **"We will be protected by the great men and women of our military and law enforcement and, most importantly, we are protected by God."**

Somewhere in that period of peace and prosperity Asa's faith in God was slowly slipping away. When the northern kingdom of Israel began to encroach on Judah's northern border, Asa stripped the treasury of the holy Temple of its silver and gold (which had been dedicated to the Lord, therefore it wasn't Asa's to give away) and he sent something that belonged to *HaShem* to the ungodly Ben Hadad, king of Aram. Asa then begged and bribed him to attack the army of Israel so it would withdraw from Judah's border.

What caused Asa's faith to slip away?
It may have been the years of peace and prosperity, when the immediacy of God's help didn't seem so necessary. Or it may have been that he surrounded himself with "yes" men and for three decades he became unaccustomed to anyone disagreeing with him. Where was the High Priest who should have been speaking against such an ungodly act? Maybe he had heard about the Johnson Amendment and was afraid to open his mouth.

It seems that Asa had gotten fat, dumb, arrogant, mean and unapproachable. It also seems reasonable to assume that he was applauded for his brilliance in hiring the army of Aram to do his fighting and how it only cost money and not the lives of Judah's boys to pull off that "clever deal." BUT, when he was confronted by Hanani the Seer (prophet) who pointedly told the king that he had made an egregious spiritual mistake by relying on a pagan ally instead of the Lord, Asa flew into a rage. He immediately had Hanani the prophet imprisoned for daring to tell him the truth. Asa compounded his problems by making more and more foolish decisions until it cost him his health and his life.

So, a king's administration that began so wonderfully ended in tragedy, regret and estrangement from his Lord. As a young leader, Asa relied fully on the Lord until he became experienced and self-sufficient. In his latter years, he must have come to believe that his success was his own doing, rather than an undeserved gift from God. He thought he could win his battles through his own power, cleverness and diplomacy. That proud self-confidence slowly led to his downfall and the oppression of his subjects.

Lesson's Learned From his Father's Career

Did Asa's son Jehoshaphat follow in his father's footsteps? Did he learn from his mistakes or did he even recognize the mistakes so that he wouldn't duplicate them? In those days, it was standard practice to cement alliances between countries by sealing the deal with a marriage between the royal families. Right into our modern times we can still see the remnants of those marriages in Europe. In the long run, these royal marriages never brought permanent peace and indeed, family rivalries often spawned additional wars. Jehoshaphat allowed his son to marry the daughter of two of the evilest of Biblical characters. His son Jehoram married the daughter of Ahab and Jezebel. Anyone with half a brain should have foreseen that nothing but evil could have been birthed out of that heifer.

It was the start of the eventual destruction and deportation of the people of Judah. To make matters worse, when Jehoshaphat allied his army with that of Ahab, many Judean fighters lost their lives in a battle that only could have benefited wicked Ahab's kingdom. Jehoshaphat not only squandered the lives of his fighting men, but he barely escaped with his own life as a result of his foolish decisions.

Now the story gets even more interesting when he is confronted (just as his father was years before) by Jehu the son of the Prophet who had been jailed by his father. (2 Chronicles 16:10).

We pick up the story in the king's palace in Jerusalem in chapter 19.

"19:1 When Jehoshaphat king of Judah returned safely to his palace in Jerusalem, 2 Jehu the seer, the son of Hanani, went out to meet him and said to the king, "Should you help the wicked and love those who hate the Lord? Because of this, the wrath of the Lord is on you. 3 There is, however, some good in you, for you have rid the land of the Asherah poles and have set your heart on seeking God."

Confronted by the prophet, Jehoshaphat listened.

The seer realized that this 'word of correction' he had fearlessly delivered, was penetrating the ego of the king. His final words were, *"you have set your heart on seeking God."*
Which he did, indeed.

In short, this is what Jehoshaphat did before he went off the rails:
1. Border Fortification
2. Religious Reform
3. National Education
4. Tax Reform
5. Military Strengthened

And now he made the most important addition to that list by listening to spiritual correction (which his father had failed to do). Just as King David had to hear a stinging rebuke from Nathan (2 Samuel 12), Jehoshaphat also needed to be told that he had acted foolishly and endangered the nation. We learn that the king was not as arrogant as his father Asa had become but was humble enough to realize that he made a serious mistake and was determined to take corrective action.

> *"19:4 Jehoshaphat lived in Jerusalem, and he went out again among the people from Beersheba to the hill country of Ephraim and turned them back to the Lord, the God of their ancestors."*

He continued to push this spiritual development for the nation even though he could have said, "Hey, I did that five years ago." No, the teachers went back at his direction and did it again. For a nation to change its basic philosophy, it likely takes a minimum of a generation being continually educated before real national change can be seen. It is not a "one and done" operation. It must be continual and consistent.

> *"5. He appointed judges in the land, in each of the fortified cities of Judah. 6. He told them, "Consider carefully what you do, because you are not judging for mere mortals but for the Lord, who is with you whenever you give a verdict. 7. Now let the fear of the Lord be on you. Judge carefully, for with the Lord our God there is no injustice or partiality or bribery."*

He realized that Judicial reform was needed and that a nation suffering under unjust laws and judges would not last long. In the US system the Supreme Court is mandated to be the impartial panel of justices who are to determine the constitutional validity of the laws passed by Congress and the conduct of the judicial system. Perhaps the most lasting impact that a president might have are his life-time appointments made to the Supreme Court.

Just four months into his presidency, President Trump's selection of Judge **Neil Gorsuch** to the Supreme Court broke a 4 - 4 stalemate on the 9-person panel. With the retirement of Justice Anthony Kennedy, President Trump nominated **Brett Kavanaugh** to the Supreme Court. The hearings for Kavanaugh were probably the most contentious in recorded US history.

Neil Gorsuch   Brett Kavanaugh

It wasn't that there was anything in his background or writings that would have disqualified him, it was just the fact that his appointment would possibly tip the court's balance to the conservative side of the scale. In addition, the advanced age of some of the justices makes it likely that President Trump will have the opportunity to appoint others, thereby transforming the court for many years in the future. The average tenure on the court has been 20 years of service .

The next reform Jehoshaphat undertook was judicial reform.
And then he was told: 2 Chron. 20: 1. *"After this..."*

The phrase 'after this' refers to the death of Ahab and the debacle of the battle on the Golan in which much of Judah's army was killed and therefore the nation's defensive ability appeared to be weakened. Neighboring enemies sensed weakness and an apparent opportunity to overrun Judah.

"After this, the Moabites and Ammonites with some from Mount Seir come to wage war against Jehoshaphat.... A vast army is coming against you from Edom, from the other side of the Dead Sea. It is already in En Gedi."

This army was much bigger than the army of Judah. When he realized the quandary he was in, look at what this leader did.

3. *"Alarmed, Jehoshaphat resolved to inquire of the Lord,"; "AND he proclaimed a fast for all Judah. The people of Judah came together... indeed, they came from every town in Judah to SEEK HIM."*
"5 Then Jehoshaphat stood up in the assembly of Judah and Jerusalem at the temple of the Lord in the front of the new courtyard and signaled "Let us pray!"

Wait a minute, isn't that what Melania did?

In Jehoshaphat's prayer, he 'reminded' God of how He had saved Israel in past history; the armies that were going to attack were those that Israel's forefathers had been merciful to in the past, according to His own specific directions (Deut. 2:9). He was not reminding God because He is forgetful, it was to remind the praying crowd and himself of how God had intervened against the inevitable and saved them in the past.
It also reminded all those listening (and us reading it right now) that we are to recall and remember to...
"Praise the Lord, ...and forget not all his benefits— He forgives.....heals... redeems... crowns... satisfies, ...renews, and provides justice. (Psalm 103)

"Forget not all the benefits that God did in the past."
He didn't recite the intelligence reports he had received, nor fearfully think or say, "We're going to be wiped out! We are going to die!"
No! He reminded God to not only build his own faith, but also that of the nation.

"Politicians can't manage. All they can do is talk."

"Lord, the God of our ancestors, are you not the God who is in heaven? You rule over all the kingdoms of the nations. Power and might are in your hand, and no one can withstand you. 7 Our God, did you not drive out the inhabitants of this land before your people Israel and give it forever to the descendants of Abraham your friend?"

What is Jehoshaphat doing?
He is pounding home the truth of the Godly Covenant as to who is entitled to the land...by Godly Decree!

"8 They have lived in it and have built in it a sanctuary for your Name, saying, 9 'If calamity comes upon us, whether the sword of judgment, or plague or famine, we will stand in your presence before this temple that bears your Name and will cry out to you in our distress, and you will hear us and save us."

Jehoshaphat is not reciting some wimpy prayer written by a speechwriter so it wouldn't offend any of his constituents. He is laying the facts (as he knows them) on the line and is asking for justice from the Righteous Judge of the world.

10 "But now here are men from Ammon, Moab and Mount Seir, whose territory you would not allow Israel to invade when they came from Egypt; so they turned away from them and did not destroy them. 11 See how they are repaying us by coming to drive us out of the possession you gave us as an inheritance. 12 Our God, will you not judge them? For we have no power to face this vast army that is attacking us. We do not know what to do..."

This nationally televised prime time speech to the nation is not an unrepentant Nixonian resignation. Nor is it an attempt to rally the troops when the chips are down. It is a politically unbelievable approach! Can you think of a world leader who would address his nation and wind it up by saying, "I don't know what to do!"
No, they always have the answer. That's why they make the big bucks.

"But our eyes are on you."
(We are going to listen to what You have to say.) Jehoshaphat made valid calculations and, realizing his vulnerability, he reminded God of His history, His promise, and of His Covenants with Israel. The king humbled himself before God (and his nation) and he waited expectantly for God to judge.

And guess what?
God spoke!

> *2 Chron. 29: 15 "Listen, King Jehoshaphat and all who live in Judah and Jerusalem! This is what the Lord says to you: 'Do not be afraid or discouraged because of this vast army. For the battle is not yours, but God's! Tomorrow march down against them. They will be climbing up by the Pass of Ziz, and you will find them at the end of the gorge in the Desert of Jeruel. 17 You will not have to fight this battle. Take up your positions; stand firm and see the deliverance the Lord will give you, Judah and Jerusalem. Do not be afraid; do not be discouraged. Go out to face them tomorrow, and the Lord will be with you.'"*

That is exactly what happened.

In the morning, Jehoshaphat put the weakest and most unlikely men he had at the head of the march. Most of them had never trained with sword or spear and were probably **4F** with flat feet. It was the Cantors who led the entire army. Maybe they fancied themselves as the Cantor Company (if they were orthodox, the *Hazzan* Platoon). He sent the unarmed singers out first, singing praises, and as the army marched out, the enthusiastic loud praises drowned out all other sounds. None of the troops could hear the sound of battle that raged between the three armies that were on their way to attack them.

4-F is a classification given to someone trying to join indicating that he or she is "not acceptable for service in the Armed Forces" due to medical, dental, or other reasons.

As a result of the ambushes being triggered by obedience to God's Order of Battle Plan, the enemies attacked each other and wiped out each of their own allied armies. By the time Israel's army got there, there was nothing to do but pick up the spoils. There was so much that it took three days of heavy lifting to accomplish the battlefield cleanup. How they must have repeated to each other "For the battle is not yours, but God's!"

What has President Trump done that makes him eligible to be included on our Rushmore collection of Presidents who have blessed the Jews and the Israeli State?

At the time this book is going to press, Donald Trump has been in office less than three years. Those incredible months were marked by a constant drumbeat of obstructionist moves by his opposition, not only from the Democratic party but also in his own Republican party. For the first time in history there was the unveiling of another anti-Trump element no one had ever heard of before. It was the "Deep State" - a slimy mixture of entrenched bureaucrats and elected politicians who act and think that they know better than the will of the American voters.

DEEP STATE: a body of people, typically influential members of government agencies or the military, believed to be involved in the secret manipulation or control of government policy. "the Deep State and its policy of allowing extremist ideologies to flourish may be the actual issues of concern".
The term was originally coined to refer to a relatively invisible state apparatus in Turkey (*derin devlet*) "composed of high-level elements within the intelligence service s, military, security, judiciary, and organized crime" and similar alleged networks in other countries including Egypt, Ukraine, Spain, Colombia, Italy, Israel, and many other.

Revelation after revelation uncovered the shocking reality that a large segment of our government was operating without any elected oversight (often ignoring legal Congressional demands) and was abusing its awesome powers in a myriad of ways. It seemed that the evil swamp could not fathom the idea that Trump had actually been elected.

It was unthinkable because he was not a charter member of the Old Swamp Club and had never before been asked to sell his soul for an elected or even an appointed position in the District of Columbia. Like Harold Hill of the Music Man, he just, "didn't know the territory."

Powerful entrenched bureaucrats and elected officials with access to Top Secret information selectively leaked damaging secrets to their trusted media friends in an attempt to undermine a president that they despised. The first years of the Trump administration were darkly overshadowed by Trump-haters searching for any kind of a misstatement, "high crime or misdemeanor" which might be used to impeach the president, or at least block every campaign promise he ever made from being enacted.

Unashamed, those deeply shocked, mortally wounded and dangerously enraged 'deep staters' kept repeating statements like the following: "It was owed to Hillary and somehow he must have stolen it by colluding with the all-powerful Russians and their puppet master Putin."
With zero evidence for Russian collusion they could have just as easily blamed the Chinese or Venezuela or the Lilliputians. "We know he did it because he's not smart enough to have honestly beaten Queen Hillary.

That's not the way you are supposed to win elections -by colluding with the electoral college. Whatever happened to the popular vote?
Well, even if the popular vote historically or unconstitutionally never was used for any presidential election, in this case it should have been because we got more votes!

Much of the charges peeped by the banty rooster Congressperson **Adam Schiff** could have been better crowed by the looney-tuned southern cartoon chicken Senator **Foghorn J. Leghorn,** who would have postulated, *"I say, I say boy, there's got to be some colludin' or obstructin' going on here in the barnyard. I say, I say it's high time we did some impeachin' in this here barnyard."*

Adam Schiff

Tip O"Neill

The real collusion, it turns out, was by the FBI, the DOJ, the CIA , HRC and the rest of the DC alphabet swamp, NOT Trump and the Russkies.

FBI - The Federal Bureau of Investigation is the domestic intelligence and security service of the United States and its principal federal law enforcement agency.

DOJ - The United States Department of Justice or Justice Department, is a federal executive department of the United States government, responsible for the enforcement of the law and administration of justice in the United States, equivalent to the justice or interior ministries of other countries.

CIA - The Central Intelligence Agency is a civilian foreign intelligence service of the federal government of the United States, tasked with gathering, processing, and analyzing national security information from around the world, primarily through the use of human intelligence

HRC - The Human Rights Council is an inter-governmental body within the United Nations system made up of 47 States responsible for the promotion and protection of all human rights around the globe. It has the ability to discuss all thematic human rights issues and situations that require its attention throughout the year. It meets at the UN Office in Geneva, Switzerland.

For many reasons, they all wanted Mr. Trump to lose the election. When he didn't oblige, they tried to remove him from office. And unfortunately for the nation, they are still trying.

Never since the days of Andrew Jackson has there been such a tenacious fighter in the Oval Office. In spite of the constant drumbeat of political opposition within and outside his own party, the accomplishments of this administration are truly unprecedented.

What did Trump do for Israel and the Jewish people that elevated him into the pantheon of presidents that blessed the Land and people of Israel?

Like so many presidential candidates since 1995, Trump also promised to recognize Jerusalem as the capital of Israel and to move the US embassy there. For more than two decades, this promise had been routinely sidestepped every six months. On the 6th of December 2017, when the president announced that he would make the move, this instantly provoked (rather muted) protests across the Middle East.

The lack of genuine outrage in the Arab street was significant compared to the world-shaking cataclysm that had been predicted if the US dared to change anything when it came to Jerusalem's status.

We were repeatedly told that to even think about making a change of the status quo, this would unleash, at a bare minimum, the third world war. Outraged Palestinian leaders indignantly blustered that the U.S. was now disqualified as a mediator in the long-stalled peace process. Not to be outdone in the outrage category, the United Nations General Assembly voted 128-9 to condemn the plan. No surprises there.

Meanwhile, within the administration the decision also sparked a battle between the State Department on the one hand and Trump, Pence and Jared Kushner on the other. Pence and Kushner, in charge of the Middle East peace process, had opted for the embassy to be moved quickly.

The Secretary of State Rex Tillerson publicly argued they would need several years to build a new embassy. Then, out of the blue, the proposed move was further clouded in confusion when an undersecretary of state said plans to build a new embassy in Jerusalem had been abandoned because such construction would be "cost-prohibitive."

> **"I like thinking big. If you're going to be thinking anything, you might as well think big." Trump**

Pence - Kushner - Tillerson

Both the Secretary and his deputy should have remembered that their boss made his career in constructing massive buildings on time and under cost. With that pronouncement, they really had stomped on the wrong toes. That same day, both cleaned out their desks and left town under a cloud of dust and a tepid, "Hi yo Silver! Away!"

On the 14th of May 2018 (the 70th anniversary of the Declaration of the State of Israel) Trump followed through on his commitment to move the US embassy from Tel Aviv to Jerusalem.

Trump's decision to recognize Jerusalem as the capital of Israel and transfer the embassy from the undisputed 'unholy city' of Tel Aviv to the holy city of Jerusalem, was a highly significant and symbolic diplomatic gesture that came without any apparent concessions from Israel. As of now, no congressman has found a *quid for a quo* to besmirch the transfer and start another impeachment. But, standby... I'm sorry I mentioned the possibility.

Quid pro quo is a Latin phrase used in English to mean an exchange of goods or service s, in which one transfer is contingent upon the other; "a favor for a favor". Phrases with similar meanings include: "give and take", "tit for tat", "you scratch my back, and I'll scratch yours", and "one hand washes the other".

The actual move enraged Palestinians and other token noises squeaked momentarily from some Arab and European allies. It reversed decades of US and international policy, which had left the future status of Jerusalem, claimed by both Israelis and Palestinians as their capital, to be settled during peace talks.

The embassy transfer and the resulting Gazan deaths from rioting and border fence attacks are some of the latest Trumpian steps that diplomats and foreign leaders say have diminished US influence on the world scene.

Typical was the statement by **Aaron David Miller,** a veteran Middle East peace negotiator,
"Rarely have I seen an administration more hostile towards the Palestinians. What we are seeing is a preternatural effort by the administration to identify itself with the state of Israel and this government of Israel."
Miller, who served under six secretaries of State in Democratic and Republican administrations, said the Trump approach was unprecedented.

For once in his long-failed career, he was right. It was unprecedented, but that did not make it wrong. All the previous approaches had miserably failed. Miller has admitted that his twenty years of being present during countless peace talks have been a failure.

He invariably points out that whatever Trump does in Israel only makes the situation worse. He never credits the president with an innovative and honest attempt at peacemaking. He always points out how each move is somehow trying to get a political advantage either for himself or his buddy Bibi. After blasting the embassy move, the Golan recognition, the 'legality' of the Jewish settlements in Judea and Samaria (West Bank), the Peace Plan, and the ensuing adjustments of the conceptual map of a Palestinian state, it is easy to predict Miller's coming critiques as time and the plan unfold.

Sadly, Miller is not a lone voice, but he does have years of inside work on the problem. Whenever anything new happens regarding the Peace Plan, you can be assured that he will be the first on the scene to point out how it is doomed to failure.

Another thing that drives Trump's critics crazy is that he has refused to totally pay homage to the hallowed and untouchable formula of "a two-state solution of Israel living in peace next to an independent Palestine," which was the long internationally accepted consensus mantra for resolving the conflict.

For Trump's evangelical pro-Israel base, any movement away from the failed antiquated formulas was truly a huge achievement. (Trump likes 'huge'). Most of those formulas have been based on maximalist Palestinian demands deemed 'holy' by the international community (which is historically anti-Israel).

> **"Part of being a winner is knowing when enough is enough. Sometimes you have to give up the fight and walk away, and move on to something that's more productive."**
>
> **"Sometimes your best investments are the ones you don't make." Trump**

The US president charged that **Mahmoud Abbas,** the PA leader,  deceived him regarding his party's (Fattah) involvement in anti-Israel incitement. Trump clearly lambasted Abbas during a meeting in Bethlehem,

"You tricked me in Washington," he yelled at Abbas. "You talked to me about peace, but the Israelis showed me that you are personally supporting incitement!"

In September of 2018, Trump went on a crusade against the Palestinian Authority by ordering the closure of the Palestine Liberation Organization office in Washington because the PLO "has not taken steps to advance the start of direct and meaningful negotiations with Israel."

Because of the continued Palestinian refusal to meet with his team tasked with seeking an Israeli-Palestinian peace deal, Trump responded by cutting vast sums of US aid to Palestinian organizations and UN groups that support Palestinians.

In an attempt to get their attention, he withdrew US funds from **UNRWA,** the UN agency for Palestinian refugees, the Palestinian Authority, the East Jerusalem hospital network, and Israeli-Palestinian co-existence programs.

UNWRA: The United Nations Relief and Works Agency for Palestine Refugees in the Near East is an UN agency created in December 1949 to support the relief and human development of Palestinian refugees

---

The president, who seems to see all foreign relations as 'deal making', knows the power of taking and leaving issues on or off the table.
The formerly untouchable issues are now very much 'touchable'. Changing the rules of the game upsets most of the players as well as those *kibitzers* offering their meddlesome advice .

Kibitzer is a Yiddish term for a spectator, usually one who offers a d v i c e   o r commentary.
The term can be applied to any activity, but is most commonly used to describe spectators in games such as contract bridge, chess and *Schafkopf.*

On 15 February 2017, during a press conference with the Israeli Prime Minister, Trump responded, *"I am looking at two-state, and one-state, and I like the one that both parties like. I'm very happy with the one that both parties like."* Trump continued, *"I can live with either one. I thought for a while the two-state looked like it may be the easier of the two. But honestly... if Israel and the Palestinians are happy, I'm happy with the one they like the best."*

What did that mean? It was earth shattering to all those invested in the failed (again and again) two-state solution. Trump actually had the temerity, gall, audacity and chutzpah to throw the liberals' most beloved peace plan under the local bus.

255

That plan first saw the light of day over 45 years ago when it surfaced in a UN Resolution, and it was resurrected time and again under various names such as Oslo, Madrid, Wye River, Camp David, etc., etc., ad nauseam.

Trump, the quintessential deal maker, knew that it was not going to happen, no matter how much lipstick you put on the porker. In a few seconds he uttered the words that junked a frequently failed *shibboleth* of the left and opened up new possibilities.

> A *shibboleth* is any custom or tradition, usually a choice of phrasing or even a single word, that distinguishes one group of people from another. In the Old Testament, shibboleth was a password used by the Israelites. It was chosen because their enemies could not pronounce it.

Any great deal maker must be ready to walk away from a bad deal. He probably realized that one side wanted it too much and the other didn't really want it at all. With that short statement he opened the door for some 'out of the box' thinking.

What a welcome change from when Obama needlessly created personal animosity between himself and the Israeli Prime Minister.

Rather than working out any policy disagreements behind closed doors in private, members of Obama's cabinet gleefully leaked insults about Netanyahu to the press. In doing so, they attempted to use pressure to force Israel to make concessions to a Palestinian Authority which refused to recognize Israel's legitimacy and repeatedly denied the Jewish people's undeniable connection to the land.

How does the Jewish Israeli population view the US policy changes?

One would expect Israeli Jews to agree on this matter. The Israelis, however, are also divided on most domestic and foreign policy issues, including the path forward on Palestinian relations. (Sound familiar?) Since Jerusalem has both religious and political significance, one would expect variations across the religious/secular divide within Judaism. But on the embassy issue, Jewish Israelis seemed to have banded together to support Trump's Embassy move. It appears that the Israeli citizens are genuinely and vociferously in agreement with the US president's moves. This attitude is in stark contrast with many Americans and indeed most people around the world, who continue to hold unfavorable views of Trump and his initiatives.

The Joint Comprehensive Plan Of Action

Trump unilaterally withdrew from the 2015 multinational deal glaringly misnamed 'The Joint Comprehensive Plan Of Action' which was somehow supposed to prevent Iran from developing nuclear weapons.
Trump terminated this plan on 8 May 2018, along with slapping extreme sanctions back on the Iranian economy.
"We cannot prevent an Iranian bomb under the decaying and rotten structure of the current agreement," the president said in justifying his decision. *"Therefore, I am announcing today that the United States will withdraw from the Iran nuclear deal."*

That unilateral move dynamically showed Israel and the world that the United States was militarily ready to defend Israel because it had been shown that, despite the Nuclear Deal, the Iranians were secretly continuing their efforts in building a nuclear weapon and its delivery system. Again, this master chess move was unilateral with no other country of significance joining in the walkout or even tepidly applauding.

> "The problems we face now - poverty and violence at home, war and destruction abroad - will last only as long as we continue relying on the same politicians who created them in the first place." Trump

But it did start a movement in some Middle Eastern Arab countries who had long recognized that their greatest threat was not from Israel but from Iran. This was a sea change that most middle east experts never saw coming. Of course they never saw Trump coming either.

The Crown Jewel

In Israel, the recognition of Jerusalem as the capital was seen as the crown jewel of a close bond forged between the US and Israel, not between Trump and Netanyahu. If it was only a pact between the leaders and not the nations it would be weak and temporary. Similar pressures on both leaders (continual investigations, indictments, impeachment, elections) can have a dampening effect on the honeymoon if the partners are changed, weakened or distracted.

As of this writing, President Trump is seen as a clear friend upon whom Israel can rely. The firm belief of strong backing of our most important and only reliable ally in the Middle East (and probably the world) extends throughout the president's Cabinet and reaches across his entire administration.

GOLAN HEIGHTS RECOGNITION

On 25 March 2019, recognition of the Golan Heights as an integral part of the nation and not subject to negotiation was an incredible reversal of policy by President Trump.

He wrote, *"After 52 years it is time for the United States to fully recognize Israel's sovereignty over the Golan Heights, which is of critical strategic and security importance to the State of Israel and regional stability!"*

That presidential proclamation made the United States the first country, other than Israel, to recognize Israeli rather than Syrian sovereignty over the Golan Heights region.

The Israel armed forces had captured the Golan from Syria in the 1967 Six-Day War. In 1981, in a move that was not internationally recognized at the time, the Government of Israel formally annexed it with the Golan Heights Law under the courageous leadership of Prime Minister Menachem Begin.

The proclamation by Trump cited, *"...aggressive acts by Iran and terrorist groups, including Hezbollah, in southern Syria, are justification for Israel to maintain sovereignty over the Golan Heights, for Israel has a need to protect itself from Syria and other regional threats."*

One of the biggest guffaws I had over this recognition by Trump of the Golan came from a Reuters article which quoted Russian state media as saying Trump's comments, "risked seriously destabilizing the region."
I guess by "region" they must mean the former nation of Syria.

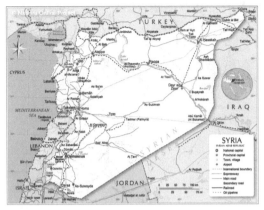 You remember Syria, don't you? It's that lovely country from which 5.7 million people fled from their homes to refugee camps outside Syria.

An estimated 6 million other Syrians are displaced into camps within their own borders. The former Syria is that wonderful country where hundreds of thousands have been killed in combat and from poisonous Sarin gas attacks. The former Syria is that delightful country where forces from Iran, Hezbollah, Russia, Turkey and numerous small terror groups have converged to join in an orgy of killing. No one knows the actual number of deaths, but it is agreed that more than 550,000 have died so far in the multi-year conflict.

Meanwhile, all the usual 'buddies', like the European Union and other countries, banded together to reject Trump's recognition of the importance of the Golan to Israel's security. After all, what are European friends for if you can't rely on them to oppose whatever you do or say?

Prior to the start of the Syrian debacle in 2011 there were numerous 'peace deals' in the offing. Previous Israeli administrations were ready to trade the Golan for a full 'normalization' with Syria.
In his spare time, when John Kerry wasn't giving trillions to the Iranian leadership, he was busy riding his other hobby horse: pushing Israel to give the Golan to the Assad dynasty. He was chasing the elusive Nobel Peace Prize to cap his illustrious career of failed deals.

Today, the 40,000 Israeli citizens and Druze residents living on the Golan Heights are thankful that those Kerry-Hillary peace dreams amounted to only a cloud of ephemeral smoke rings.

Imagine the chaos if those terrorist units had taken over the high ground commanding all of Israeli Galilee.

Former Israeli Prime Minister **Ehud Olmert** appeared ready to make the deal several times before he left office and entered prison.
His unbelievable offer to Palestinian Authority chairman Mahmoud Abbas  included the entire area of Judea and Samaria, eastern Jerusalem as their capital and placing the entire Old City of Jerusalem, including the Western Wall, under international control.

It was a last ditch offer, as Olmert was packing his undies for a long stay in prison, when he offered all of the above as a Palestinian State. Olmert probably realized that he was massively over-stepping his authority with that offer but playing loose with the niceties of the law had become his way of life. But it proves to what extremes one will go to avoid a prison cell. He eventually served 16 months of a 27-month sentence for fraud and bribery.

As another failed peacemaker who continues to get lots of media attention, he is of course opposed to Trump's plan. His latest gambit is to meet the master Peace-Avoider Mahmoud Abbas at the UN in New York and hold joint press conferences to attack the Plan and Trump and Netanyahu. I think both of them could easily be hired as staff experts on either MSNBC or CNN.

Will President Trump be lured by the seductive siren call that caused the shipwrecks of ancient Greek mariners as he chases 'Deals' never done before, such as ones with North Korea, Russia or China?
Could he be misled like Jehoshaphat appeared to have been after so much success?

How can we be Involved?

Do we Have the Right to Involve Ourselves in the Current Administration?

I'm glad you asked those questions.

We not only have the **right** - we have the **responsibility** and the **assigned mission orders**!

The apostle Paul advised Christians who wondered what to think of the governments they themselves were living under,
"Therefore I exhort first of all that supplications, prayers, intercessions, and giving of thanks be made for all men, for kings and all who are in authority, that we may lead a quiet and peaceable life in all godliness and reverence."
(1 Timothy 2:1-2, emphasis added).

Any nation will ultimately be humbled or destroyed for its evil treatment of God's people Israel. When Egypt was doing it, God sent Moses to tell Pharaoh,
"Indeed for this purpose I have raised you up, that I may show My power in you, and that My name may be declared in all the earth." (Exodus 9:16).

Daniel stated,
"Praise the name of God forever and ever ... He controls the course of world events; he removes kings and sets up other kings"
(Daniel 2:20-21.)

Daniel also stated,
"So that the living may know [without any doubt] That the Most High [God] rules over the kingdom of mankind And He bestows it on whomever He desires And sets over it the humblest and lowliest of men." (Daniel 4:17 AMP)

262

The apostle Paul, writing to Christians living in the capital city of the Roman Empire, wrote,

"All authority comes from God, and those in positions of authority have been placed there by God." (Romans 13:1, see also Psalms 75:6-7; John 19:10-11).

Scripture shows that sometimes God does intervene and decides who will be the leading official of a nation. He also allows the citizens to pick their national leaders whose values are not aligned with Scripture.

Hosea 8:4 says,

"Israel has rejected the good...they set up kings, but not by me."

It seems a clear lesson that God only approves of those rulers who have not "rejected the good" as defined by the Lord.

Ezekiel 22:30 (NIV) says, *"I looked for someone among them who would build up the wall and stand before me in the gap on behalf of the land so I would not have to destroy it, but I found no one."*

Proverbs 21:1 *"The king's heart is a stream of water in the hand of the Lord; he turns it wherever he will."*

Romans 13:1 *"Let every person be subject to the governing authorities. For there is no authority except from God, and those that exist have been instituted by God."*

Daniel 2:21 *"It is He who changes the times and the epochs; He removes kings and ... It is God who alters the times and seasons, and he removes kings and promotes kings."*

Remember the story of Jehoshaphat?

We saw the remarkable changes he instituted in making the Kingdom of Judah great again.

Did Jehoshaphat have a weakness? Yes, it seemed he wanted to cozy up to the northern kings of Israel. It seems that he was always ready to "do a deal" with some very untrustworthy and godless characters.

Jehoshaphat made an alliance with the wicked king Ahab and almost lost his life and did lose much of his army. Later he went into business with Ahab's wicked son and lost his costly fleet. Scripture doesn't tell us what his motivation was or why he had that overwhelming desire to be Bob Barker shouting, "Let's make a Deal!" (Yeah, I know it was Mnty Hall. I just wanted to see if you were still awake.)

 Robert William Barker is a retired American television game show host. He is known for hosting CBS's "The Price Is Right" from 1972 to 2007, making it the longest-running daytime game show in North American television history. He is also known for hosting "Truth or Consequences" from 1956 to 1974.

Each of those alliances backfired on him and weakened his army, treasury and country.

Because of his diplomatic and deal-making skills, Jehoshaphat had established good relations with the northern kingdom of Israel, a frequent threatening neighbor. To make the deal of a lifetime and cement good relations he agreed to a marriage between his son Prince Jehoram and Princess Athaliah, daughter of Israel's King Ahab and his missus, the incredibly wicked Jezebel. This was certainly against the Lord's wishes, for God forbids marriages — and indeed all partnerships — between His people and those who are committed to evil.

In a short period of time, Trump has brought more change to our nation than even FDR did at the beginning of his first term in 1933 during the depths of the Great Depression.

At the beginning of May 2018, the Israeli Prime Minister presented to the world a treasure trove of nuclear files smuggled out of Iran by the Mossad, purporting to show Iran's nuclear intentions and past preparations for a weapon to be used against Israel. It was a

blockbuster intelligence coup. What was publicly revealed was a synopsis of the documents and files consisting of 100,000 pages regarding Iran's lying about their nuclear weapons program during a four-year period.

Within a week of Netanyahu's public revelation President Trump also acted. He went against the caution of his own CIA chief, Director **Gina Haspel,** and US Intelligence Director **Dan Coats**. Both testified that they didn't have conclusive proof of Iran's nuclear intentions. As usual, Trump had his own gut instincts and perhaps some other

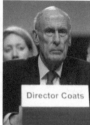

Gina Haspel and Dan Coats

evidence. Recalling numerous past intel failures, he went with his own 'elected' judgment and made a startling pronouncement from the Oval Office on the 8th of May 2018. By using the presidential prerogative of Executive Memorandum, he withdrew our government from the Joint Comprehensive Plan of Action (JCPOA).

JCPOA, better known as the "Iranian Deal', was technically never a legitimate treaty.

The Joint Comprehensive Plan of Action, known commonly as the Iran nuclear deal or Iran deal, is an agreement on the Iranian nuclear program reached in Vienna on July 14, 2015, between Iran and the P5+1 together with the European Union.

President Obama used an Executive Agreement to get the US membership in the European gang of businessmen salivating about the likelihood of making business deals with the pious religious and utterly trustworthy leadership in Teheran.

> **"I have embraced crying mothers who have lost their children because our politicians put their personal agendas before the national good. I have no patience for injustice, no tolerance for government incompetence, no sympathy for leaders who fail their citizens." Trump**

The billions of dollars delivered on the tarmac in the dark of night, on countless pallets, was quickly disbursed to Iranian-controlled terror groups. By stating that the payoff was billions of dollars in cash, Trump was derided by his enemies as "someone who knows nothing about money." Isn't it interesting that one of the richest businessmen in the world got there by knowing nothing about money?

Trump unilaterally imposed unprecedented sanctions on Iran and those who trade with the "Mother of all world-wide Terrorism".
He did it by an Executive Memorandum, solemnly signed in the Oval Office to cease US participation in the JCPOA and to deny Iran all paths to a Nuclear Weapon. In the background the screeching strains of whining and moaning could be heard coming from the All-European Complaints Choir in the key of C (cash).

The reality is that Trump's undercutting and slowing of the Iranian nuclear program is another blessing for Israel. He had to do it unilaterally because no one else in Europe or the UN dared to take the lead in doing what was right.

Nevertheless, it was Barack Obama's failure to seek ratification from Congress that allowed President Trump to end it so quickly and unilaterally.

What the executive order pen can give, the same pen in the hand of a succeeding executive can take away. To quote the 44th president, **_"Elections have consequences."_**

Throughout 2018 and 2019 Trump's peace team — led by his son-in-law and senior adviser Jared Kushner and former special envoy Jason Greenblatt — have signaled that the publication of its proposal was imminent. Sadly or happily, 'imminent' had been postponed time and again. There is no doubt that plenty of work and many changes had to be factored into it so that it wouldn't be DOA on delivery day.

Jason Greenblatt

> **DOA** stands for "dead on arrival", or "deteriorate On Approach" which is a medical and crime term used to refer to a person who was already dead when EMTs or police arrived at a scene.
> **DOA** can also mean Department of Administration.

For many years everyone was kept in the dark as to what the plan would actually entail. Parts of it were being periodically shopped around to allies, but very little leaked, and it appears to have been given a number of overhauls. It was hoped that the Trump plan would not parrot the stale Bush 1/Clinton/Bush 2/Obama parameters of yesteryear or that he would not force any 'peace paradigm' on Israel, especially not with Iran continuing its nuclear pursuit and its dogged quest for regional domination.

There was much hope and prayer that the Trump team understood that Israel can no longer make unilateral concessions in a situation where the Palestinians refuse to participate in the diplomatic process and show no capacity or inclination for any meaningful compromises whatsoever.

The economic part of the "Peace to Prosperity" plan was previewed in late June 2019 in Bahrain.

The proposal was to raise 50 billion from donors.

It was notionally broken down as follows: $28 billion would go toward the West Bank and Gaza Strip while $7.5 billion would go to Jordan, $9 billion to Egypt and $6 billion to Lebanon with economic projects and new industry scattered in those countries.

Of course, the press panned it as a dream of Trump's son-in-law and without even reading the two large documents that accompanied this part of the plan, the 'usual suspects' attempted to tear it apart.

The Palestinian leadership was represented by no one, while numerous Arab countries sent emissaries.

Trump is the first president to recognize that the Israeli-Palestinian conflict is not the root cause of the turbulence in the Middle East and is by no means the center piece of Arab policy makers. Most likely some of the delay in releasing the "Peace Plan" was because he recognizes that the region is not ripe for an imposed resolution of the problem and there is no indication that it will get any riper. Frankly, it is hard to imagine that it will ever be ready if the Palestinians are incapable of the smallest genuine compromise.

At first, the Plan appeared to be a 'take it or leave it' deal. But after nearly three years of drawing it up with some consultation from Israel, it still wasn't ready for primetime. The maps (a new innovation at the start of negotiations) were confusing and inaccurate. Those maps needed to be re-drafted and updated. Making a so-called Palestinian "state" out of the puzzle pieces of Arab and Jewish communities would be the herculean task of the initial four years allotted to the job, even if both sides were cooperating.

But it was apparent to the general public (and evidently not to the Israeli consultants) that some of the initial assumptions were dangerous to the survivability of the Jewish communities. Because the Palestinian leadership refused to acknowledge that a plan had even been offered, they had forfeited their ability to give input at the beginning of the deal.

However, one of the pieces of the plan that will not be changed is the element of defensible Israeli borders. There is no doubt that Israel must and will annex an eastern defensible topographical border. In simple terms that means that Israel will annex the widest interpretation of the Jordan Valley into the state - not just the riverbank but the steep hills, cliffs and embankments overlooking the famous stream. Controlling the high ground ensures that armies from the east cannot again have a free pass through the Hashemite kingdom into *Eretz Ysrael*. The strengthening of the eastern border and its annexation would be a great gain, even if the other elements of the plan aren't enacted, such as the demilitarization of a proposed Palestinian state.

In response to valid criticism of the Trump Plan twelve days after the

unveiling, on 9 February 2020, US Ambassador to Israel, **David Friedman,** hurriedly cautioned the Israeli government not to unilaterally rush the annexation of Israeli settlements.

That warning was in direct contrast to earlier guidance on 28 January at the White House that implied the US had given the green light to immediate unilateral annexation.

David Melech Friedman

What would have happened if the caretaker Israeli government gone ahead and annexed the Jordan River Valley under the indicted acting PM Netanyahu? If Bibi had won the election, President Trump's enemies would have used this to start another impeachment round, claiming that the Plan was a political gift to Netanyahu. Netanyahu was coming up for re-election within a few weeks, while four days previously, President Trump had been acquitted from an impeachment trial. The impeachment charges had been based on a 30-minute presidential phone call that had been interpreted by his enemies as asking a foreign government for internal political help.

Ambassador Friedman attempted to diplomatically wiggle out of a tight corner by disavowing that the Plan was a political gift to Netanyahu who had failed to be re-elected in two previous attempts. Of course, it appeared that Netanyahu's party was the choice of the administration and could be construed as a payoff. Unfortunately, the Ambassador kept referring to the "Plan" as a "Gift."

"This plan is not a gift to a political leader," he said. *"This is a gift to Israel, a gift to the Palestinians and a gift to the region. It works for everyone … Let's just give it time … Stay tuned,"* said Friedman on 9 February.

Why Trump Deserves to be Elevated to the Israeli Rushmore Quintet of Presidential Blessers of Israel

1. Trump's decision to recognize Jerusalem as the capital of Israel by moving the US Embassy to the city which had long ago been designated as such by God Himself.

2. Trump recognized Israeli sovereignty over the strategic high ground of the Golan Heights, which guards the Sea of Galilee, the farms and cities of northern Israeli and the extremely important water sources and aqueducts.

3. Trump recognized the Israeli settlements in Judea and Samaria as 'legal' and consistent with international law and not 'the illegal Jewish settlements in the Occupied West Bank'.

4. Trump unveiled 'Peace to Prosperity: A Vision to Improve the Lives of the Palestinian and Israeli People.' That plan sounded the death knell for all previous peace plan assumptions and drove a stake through the heart of the often failed formula mis-named the "two state solution."

5. Trump signed an executive order highlighting Title VI of the Civil Rights Act which will financially punish college campuses for allowing anti-Jewish and anti-Israel activity on campuses that receive Federal assistance.

6. Trump's administration reached back 100 years to the **San Remo Conference** following the 1919 Peace Talks in Paris, when the World War I victors divided up the Middle East and assigned borders to the Palestine Mandate which eventually became Israel. It was discovered that a proper understanding of the legalities of the League of Nations mandate specifies that the so-called West Bank of Israel is within the legal boundaries and legal rights of the current state of Israel. Those rights were assumed by the United Nations when it replaced the League of Nations following World War II. Trump is the first world leader that is refusing to subordinate Israel's legal rights to political blackmail from Israel's enemies.

> **The San Remo Conference** was an international meeting of the post-World War I Allied Supreme Council, held from 19 to 26 April 1920. The San Remo Resolution determined the allocation of Class "A" League of Nations mandates for the administration of three then-undefined Ottoman territories in the Middle East: "Palestine", "Syria" and "Mesopotamia". The boundaries of the three territories were "to be determined [at a later date] by the Principal Allied Powers", leaving the status of outlying areas such as Zor and Transjordan unclear.

7.   Trump's withdrawal from the JCPOA and the subsequent tariffs slapped back on Iran which will weaken their nuclear program and the underwriting of numerous terrorist groups all aimed at the elimination of Israel.

8.   Trump's defunding of The United Nations Relief and Works Agency for Palestine Refugees in the Near East (UNRWA).

9.   Trump's imposition of financial sanctions on the Palestinian Authority, especially the 'Pay for Slay' payments by the PA to families of the killers and suicide bombers of Jews.

 Mohammad Abu Shahin's parents in their home in the Qalandia refugee camp, near Ramallah. Their 32-year-old son was convicted of killing Danny Gonen. While in jail, the family collects a monthly payment from Palestinian authorities to cover the costs of their food, rent and other expenses. These controversial "salaries" are paid to prisoners and their families, both in and out of jails, as well as to the loved ones of Palestinian "martyrs" [terrorists] who have been killed by Israelis.

10. Trump's authorization of the killing of Qassem Soleimani, the leader of the Islamic Revolutionary Guard Corps' elite Quds Force, with responsibility for Iran's clandestine operations overseas, responsible for extending Iran's military reach deep into foreign conflicts like those in Syria and Iraq.

It seems that the boy from Queens and his 'New York Values' understands and reflects the values of 'Smalltown and Flyover America' more than the east and left coast liberal bastions. Who would have thought that a billionaire with bleached hair and a fake tan could be so loved by farmers, ranchers, Christians, blue collar workers and even dues-paying union members?

"You know the funny thing, I don't get along with rich people. I get along with the middle class and the poor people better than I get along with the rich people."

Trump

Well, it happened. (To everyone's surprise.) Who would have thought that so much could have been accomplished for the good of our country and Israel with so much non-stop opposition from Democrats (which was expected)?

But the Never-Trumpers, pseudo-Republicans in the House and Senate (Take a bow, Romney, Sessions, Ryan, et al.) and the 26 Republicans that retired before the 2018 mid-terms certainly made the job that much more difficult. The achieved results are therefore that much more remarkable.

Thus far, it has been an amazing ride. Pray for your leader and for his appointments that he will look to the Lord God (Who put him in that seat) for guidance and decisions.

I thank God for all the presidents who have stood strong for the basic Godly principles that our country was founded on who understood the importance of bolstering the people and the land of Israel so that it would become clear to all of those in governmental positions, elected and unelected that they too can stand for those principles as well, no matter what their position is.

And I thank God for President Trump and his family and pray for that family – that God's blessing may continue to be upon him and that he will have the wisdom to accept the advice to stand firm on God's Word.

And last, but not least, I pray for YOU, the reader. I pray that this message will resonate in your heart and mind.

I pray that YOU will take that next little step of faith that will align yourself with that great promise of Genesis 12:3.

"In the end, you're measured not by how much you undertake but by what you finally accomplish."

Trump

Donald John Trump: June 14, 1946 in New York City
45th President of the United States - Assumed office January 20, 2017
Spouse: **Melania Knauss** (m. 2005) Melania grew up in Slovenia, worked as a fashion model in Europe, became a permanent resident of the USA in 2001. Obtained U.S. citizenship in 2006 and is the first naturalized U.S. citizen to become First Lady of the United States.

Victory comes from finding opportunities in problems.

Sun Tzu

"The problems we face now - poverty and violence at home, war and destruction abroad - will last only as long as we continue relying on the same politicians who created them in the first place." Trump

Zion's Watchmen

Our ministry, "Zion's Watchmen", is based on Isaiah 62:1

*"For Zion's sake I will not keep silent,
and for Jerusalem's sake
I will not keep quiet."*

Traditionally, watchmen have stood on the ramparts of their city, peering out at the landscape.

The moment they saw danger coming, they alerted the populace and the militia.

That is one of the missions we as Zion's Watchmen have for our own nation and especially as it relates to Israel.

We are calling out to all who listen and who seriously observe what Scripture says. We also remind them of what happened to other empires.

Nations truly are judged by God when they violate His principles as they relate to Zion.

♦ We want you to be a watchman on the wall.
♦ We want you to stand up and say what the Word of God says and to warn our elected leaders: "Don't step over those lines. Stop this deadly game of pushing for a Palestinian State that would divide the land."
♦ We are to speak out. That has been the problem for Christians around the world in the last 20, 30, 40, and 50 years.

My mother always told me: "Johnny, don't talk about religion and don't talk about politics with people."

"Sorry, mom! That's all I talk about, because they are intertwined."

If your beliefs from Scripture don't affect your politics, you are missing the boat. What makes you think they can be separated? They are inevitably linked together.

We will continue to do our very best to speak to Power, to the White House, to Congress, to city and county governments, to school boards, etc. I believe that God has people who are waiting to hear and others who are already listening and just need us to wake them up.

We are to speak out for Zion's sake. Isaiah 62:1 says, *"For Zion's sake I will not keep silent, and for Jerusalem's sake I will not keep quiet."*

Our nation's present and future well-being is linked to our attitude towards Israel, which actually is our attitude toward God.

The Jewish people must be important to you! Our wellbeing as individuals is also linked to how we stand on God's word, as is the future of our nation.

America stands with Israel because her cause is our cause, her values are our values, and her fight is our fight.
— Vice President Mike Pence

Zion's Watchmen TOURS

Come and visit the Land that God calls, "My Land"!

Because of the total immersion in the land and the culture where the Bible was written, these tours have often been described as "life changing". Be assured: this trip will definitely change the way that you read and understand your Bible. While visiting the authentic places, John Somerville, David Simmons and other Israeli experts will teach about the Biblical culture. This Bible-based tour will also equip you to better understand the geo-political current (and future) events as you meet the people and hear from some world-renowned experts that visit us.

> **WARNING:** Visiting Israel can be life-changing and dangerous to all your future vacation plans (Cancun will lose its luster). It is more than likely that your heart will be touched and you fall in love with the Land and the People that God calls, "My Land" and "My Chosen people."

Zion's Watchmen Tours are led and organized by John Somerville and his Ministry partner, David Simmons.

"Zion's Watchmen's" Co-Director and Vice president David Simmons has been a minister for over 40 years. He also served as the National Cowboy Church Coordinator for CUFI.

John and David travel extensively to countries that are affected by the events in the Middle East.

Tour contact information:

⇒ Telephone: +1 559-877-2882.

Mobile (559) 760-5410

⇒ Email: israel4somerville@gmail.com

⇒ Website: israelsomerville.com

Israel TV Network

You can watch John Somerville's teaching on this subject (and many others) by visiting the website of Israel TV Network Channel.
Website: https://israeltvnetwork.tv

The network offers a variety of television programs dedicated to sharing the teachings of the Bible, love for the Jewish People, and support for the land of Israel. The programs come from both Jewish and Christian teachers dedicated to the authentic message of the Bible.

John's teachings are part of a series called "The White House and Israel". He also speaks about the "Muddled Middle East". *The Hidden Root causes of the Holocaust and anti-Semitism* and *The Rise and Fall of the British Empire* are now available as a book.

Save a Child's Heart (SACH)

Zion's Watchmen sponsors the SACH organization.
SACH patients are brought to Israel to be treated at the
Wolfson Medical Center in Holon.

Approximately 50% of the children are from the Palestinian Authority, Jordan, Iraq and Morocco; more than 30% are from Africa; and the remaining are from Asia, Eastern Europe and the Americas.

To date, SACH has treated more than 2,900 children suffering from congenital and rheumatic heart disease, aged 0 to 18 years of age from 43 countries.

For more info, please visit website: www.saveachildsheart.org

We put our heart into saving a child's life

EZRA INTERNATIONAL

Zion's Watchmen is affiliated with Ezra International, an organization based on Isaiah 11:12,

"And He will lift up a standard for the nations and assemble the banished ones of Israel, and will gather the dispersed of Judah from the four corners of the earth."

EZRA's goal is the Rescue, Return and Restoration of poor Jewish People to Israel.

Ezra International is a Christian non-profit organization that helps the poorest of the poor Jewish people make Aliyah (emigrate to Israel). The return of Jewish people to Israel today is a fulfillment of God's Promise made centuries ago. For 2,000 years, it seemed impossible. But now it's happening and scripture also promised that you can be a part of it! Read More.

Ezra's Logo: God is at the center of it all and He is reaching out to the four corners of the earth. He is re-gathering His people back to Israel and you can help provide a light to show the way home.

For more info, please visit website: www. ezrainternational.org

ABOUT JOHN AND MARY SOMERVILLE

Col. John Somerville USMC (ret.) is Director of "Zion's Watchmen", a non-profit ministry registered in Texas, USA.

A graduate of both the Naval and Army War Colleges, John earned a Ph.D. from Ohio State University. During his military active duty, he served in many countries around the world.

John's interest in the Middle East has taken him into the region more than 90 times over the past 40 years. During this time, he has led many tour groups to Israel, coached Israeli youth baseball camps and volunteered on numerous archaeological digs.

Meanwhile, Mary was fighting the battles of the home front while raising their own fire-team of six little warriors.

Through lectures, TV broadcasts and other media, John diligently works to build understanding and support for Israel. By utilizing supporters, John and Mary and their partners hope to impact American foreign policy by communicating a pro-Israel perspective to our elected officials.

Zion's Watchmen is committed to the Biblical mandate to bless, speak out and stand with Israel and the Jewish people.

John and Mary (married for 50+ years), make their home on a ranch in North Fork, California, USA.

SELECTED BIBLIOGRAPHY

The Gifts of the Jews
Cahill, Thomas
Doubleday (New York, 1998)

The Trials of Zion
Dershowitz, Alan M.
Grand Central Pub. (New York, 2010)

War in the Holy Land from Megiddo to the West Bank
Duncan, Andrew and Opatowski, Michel
Sutton Publishing (Hong Kong, 1998)

Old Testament Bible History
Edersheim, Alfred

From the Ends of the Earth: The Jews in the Twentieth Century
Gilbert, Martin
Polo Pub. (London, 1997)

The Fight for Jerusalem
Gold, Dore
Regnery Publishing, Inc. Washington, DC, 2007)

The Battle for Jerusalem
Gur, Mordechai
Popular Library (Brooklyn, N.Y., 1973)

Like Dreamers
Halevi, Yossi Klein
Harper Collins (New York, 2013)

Paris 1919
MacMillan, Margaret
Random House (New York, 2003)

Israel God's Key
Josephson, Elmer A.
Bible Light Pub. (Hillsboro, Kansas, 1974)

Jewish Roots
Juster, Dan
Destiny Image (Shippensburg, PA 1995)

The Jewish Book of Why
Kolatch, Alfred J.
Penguin Group (New York, 2003)

What is a Jew?
Kertzer, Rabbi Morris
Macmillan Pub. (New York, 1960)

A Middle East Mosaic - Fragments of Life, letters and history
Lewis, Bernard
Random House (New York, 2000)

Churchill's Promised Land-Zroman and Statecraft
Makovsky, Michael
Yale University Press (New Haven, 2007)

The Rothschilds
Morton, Frederic
Crest Book (New York, 1961)

1948 – The First Arab – Israeli War
Morris, Benny
Yale University Press (New Haven, 2008)

The Genesis Record
Morris, Henry M
Baker Book House (Grand Rapids, Mich. 1976)

Hamas Jihad
Ne'eman, Yisrael
White Hart Pub (USA 2016)

Ally, My Journey across the American-Israeli Divide
Oren, Michael B.
Random House (New York, 2015)

The Paradise of God
Ollison, Larry
Harrison House Pub. (Tulsa, Oklahoma, 2014)

Why the Jews?
Prager, Dennis and Telushkin, Joseph Simon and Schuster (New York, 2003)

The Stones Cry Out
Price, Randall
Harvest House (Eugene, 1977)

A Safe Haven
Radosh, Allis and Radosh, Ronald
Harper Collins (New York, 2009)

One Palestine Complete, Jews and Arabs under the British Mandate
Segev, Tom
Henry Holt & Company (New York, 1999)

Start-Up Nation
Senor, Dan and Singer, Saul
Hatchette Book Group (New York, 2009)

Why Israel Matters to You
Spero, Aryeh
Evergreen Press (Mobile, 2015)

The New Strong's Complete Dictionary of Bible Words
Strong, James
Thomas Nelson Pub. (Nashville, Tenn., 1996)

Bible and Sword
Tuchman, Barbara W.
Ballantine Books (New York, 1984)

Jerusalem as Jesus Knew it - Archaeology as Evidence
Wilkinson, John
Thames and Hudson (Yugoslavia, 1988)

The Prime Ministers
Avner, Yehuda
Toby Press (New Milford, CT, 2010)

The Gifts of the Jews
Cahill, Thomas
Doubleday (New York, 1998)

The Trials of Zion
Dershowitz, Alan M. Grand Central Pub. (New York, 2010)

War in the Holy Land from Megiddo to the West Bank
Duncan, Andrew and Opatowski, Michel Sutton Publishing (Hong Kong, 1998)

A Dictionary of Jewish Names and Their History
Kaganoff, Benzion
Schocken Books (New York, 1977)

A Middle East Mosaic - Fragments of Life, letters and history
Lewis, Bernard
Random House (New York, 2000)

Why are Jews Liberal?
Podhoretz, Norman
Doubleday, Random House (New York, 2009)

The Lion's Gate
Pressfield, Steven
Penguin Group (New York, 2014)

Why Israel Matters to You
Spero, Aryeh
Evergreen Press (Mobile, 2015)

Throughout history we have seen that nations were judged, are being judged, and are going to be judged on their treatment of what God calls, "My people Israel". This book is an in-depth study of the rise and fall of the British Empire. We learn what happens to a nation that chooses not to heed Genesis 12:3, "I will bless those who bless you [Abraham and his descendants], and the one who curses you I will curse." Instead of being a blessing to the apple of God's eye, they became a curse.

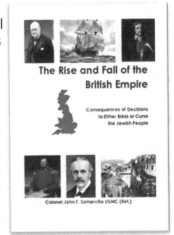

The Rise and Fall of the British Empire

Consequences of Decisions to Either Bless or Curse the Jewish People

Colonel John T. Somerville USMC (Ret.)

ISBN   9789657542781
Copyright   John T. Somerville (Standard Copyright License)
Publisher   Tsur Tsina Publications
Published   October 16, 2018
Pages   120
Binding   Perfect-bound Paperback

ORDER INFORMATION:

www.lulu.com/shop/colonel-john-t-somerville-usmc-ret/the-rise-and-fall-of-the-british-empire/paperback/product-23837367.html

Today, many churches are silent
when Israel and the Jews are
attacked vocally or physically.
Many congregations don't know a
thing about Israel being related to
God's Word. This book clarifies
how Replacement Theology, Anti-
Semitism, and the Holocaust are
horribly and intricately linked to
each other. We must realize that
the demonic forces which caused
the Holocaust are still alive and at
work. In order not to be impacted
and overwhelmed by
Replacement Theology, we must

understand where it came from, recognize its disguises and take a
vocal, personal and unwavering stand against it.

ISBN   9789657542712

Copyright   John T. Somerville (Standard Copyright License)

Publisher   Tsur Tsina Publications

Published   February 16, 2019

Pages   108

Binding   Perfect-bound Paperback

ORDER INFORMATION:

https://www.lulu.com/en/us/shop/colonel-john-t-somerville-usmc-ret/
the-hidden-root-causes-of-the-holocaust/paperback/product-
1p7r8gvp.html